THE ROMANOVS
& MR GIBBES

First published in 2002 by
Short Books
15 Highbury Terrace
London N5 1UP

10 9 8 7 6 5 4 3 2 1

A CIP catalogue record for this book
is available from the British Library.

ISBN 1-904095-16-X

Printed in England by Mackays of Chatham plc,
Chatham, Kent

THE ROMANOVS & MR GIBBES

The story of the Englishman who taught the children of the last Tsar

FRANCES WELCH

✳ **SHORT BOOKS**

To my mother and father

Sydney Gibbes circa 1930

In late May 1918 snow still covered the Siberian town of Ekaterinburg; 'snow & dirt lying' as the Tsarina noted baldly in her diary. In fact, from inside, the snow would have been barely discernible: the windows of the house in which she and her family were held had been whitewashed to prevent the captives making signals to the outside world. The Tsarina had watched in dismay as an elderly man painted over the outside panes. She recorded her displeasure with the result: '...only at the top can see a bit of sky & looks as tho' there were a thick fogg [sic], not at all cosy.' The curtains remained closed throughout the day against the glare of the sun.

The House of Special Purpose, in which the Tsar, Tsarina and their five children spent the last two months of their lives, had been requisitioned from a wealthy Ekaterinburg merchant named Ipatiev. It was a two-storey dwelling with a small garden, now surrounded by a 14-foot board fence. The family were allowed outside twice a day, for half an hour. The orders were that the windows be kept closed at all times. The Grand Duchess Anastasia tried to open one window and was shot at by a Bolshevik guard; the bullet lodged in the woodwork beside her.

The airless atmosphere in the house had a debilitating effect upon the Tsarina; she was beset with dizziness and headaches. Her sickness was compounded by her anxiety for her son, the Tsarevich Alexis. Alexis, a haemophiliac, had fallen on the day of his arrival at Ekaterinburg. He was in terrible pain. On 23 May the Tsarina wrote: 'Baby [her name for Alexis] woke up every hour from pain in his knee. Slipped & hurt when getting into bed. Cannot walk yet, one carries him.' The next day she wrote: 'Baby... suffers very much.'

In despair, the Romanovs' faithful doctor wrote a passionate appeal to the Chairman of the Ural Regional Soviet Executive Committee asking them to allow Alexis to see his English tutor, Sydney Gibbes. 'The boy is in such indescribable pain day and night that no one from among his closest relatives... has the strength to bear looking after him for long,' he wrote. 'Both teachers [Sydney Gibbes and his Swiss colleague Pierre Gilliard] are completely irreplaceable for Alexis Nikolaivich and I as a doctor must admit that they sometimes bring more relief to the patient than medical means... I write with the fervent plea that Mr Gibbes and Mr Gilliard be allowed to continue their selfless service to Alexis Nikolaivich Romanov... Do not refuse admittance to them.'

As a result of the doctor's plea, four Bolshevik officials came to examine Alexis. The rejection from the Commandant was cold:

RESOLUTION: Having examined the present request of Doctor Botkin, I think that even one servant would be one too many, because the children [Alexis' four older sisters, the Grand Duchesses Olga, Tatiana, Marie and Anastasia] can look after the patient... I suggest that the chair of the Ural Regional Soviet immediately notify these ladies and gentlemen that they have overstepped their bounds.

Sydney Gibbes was equally urgent in his efforts to be reunited with the family. He had taught the children for ten years. He had followed the family into exile after the revolution and spent seven months living with them in Tobolsk. His last view of the children had been from a window of the train in which they had all travelled to Ekaterinburg:

> The Imperial children were jostled out of the train, each being compelled to carry their own things. Nagorny [Alexis' sailor assistant] who tried to help them, was roughly handled. We could only watch from our own railway carriage window and say a silent prayer.

After the separation, Gibbes and several other members of the entourage were obliged to spend several days living in their railway carriage at Ekaterinburg station. From this unlikely base, he made repeated appeals to the authorities, stressing that he was a foreigner and technically a free man. Every day he visited the British and Swedish consuls in Ekaterinburg; he was not convinced by their assurances that the Romanovs were in no immediate danger.

One day he saw Nagorny and the grand duchesses' assistant being arrested by Red Guards outside the house; he was filled with foreboding: 'I was walking with Derevenko [another doctor] and Gilliard... when we suddenly noticed that Nagorny and Sednev, surrounded by soldiers, were leaving the House of Special Purpose. We followed them and saw that they were taken to prison,' he wrote. Nagorny and Sednev, it transpired, had tried to interfere when the guards confiscated a gold chain with holy images belonging to Alexis. They were both shot shortly afterwards.

The tutor spent his spare moments pacing up and down outside the house, gazing up in frustration at the painted windows. 'I passed the Ipatiev House many times hoping to see even a glimpse of its captives, but in vain,' he wrote. 'Only once did I see a woman's hand opening an upper window. I guessed it was the hand of the faithful lady's maid of the Empress.'

Just two months after Doctor Botkin had made his impassioned plea, the Tsar, Tsarina, their five children and four retainers, including the doctor himself, were murdered. They had been told they were to be moved to a safer location. In the early hours of the morning of 17 July 1918 they gathered in the cellar where they were told to line up against a wall for a photograph. The killing lasted 20 minutes as bullets ricocheted off the jewels that the young grand duchesses had sewn into their corsets.

***

Sydney Gibbes was appointed English tutor to the Tsar's children in 1908. Aged 32, he was tall, with scrupulously combed hair and perfect sallow skin. His full mouth had a downward cast which appeared at once melancholy and severe. When photographed he would turn his face to the right, perhaps out of vanity. His intent grey eyes, gazing upward and into the distance, would glint with a suggestion of romance.

His fastidiousness with regard to his appearance was matched by a certain stiffness of manner. In one photograph, taken in about 1911, he and his two fellow tutors are enjoying a meal outside with the Tsarevich. His colleagues are, like him, impeccably dressed; but, unlike him, they appear relaxed: one leans forward towards the table, the other wields a fork. Gibbes himself looks warily into the camera;

he sits bolt upright, his hands pressed into his lap.

Gibbes appeared an embodiment of self-restraint, a sort of Soames Forsyte. Soames developed a grim mistrust of cheerful people: he felt they were going against the facts. The appeal of such good looks as he had was undermined by his air of awkward propriety. However, Gibbes' mastery of his outward person masked an inner ferment. In another trait shared with Soames, he had an uncertain grasp of the spiritual and emotional aspects of his life. He fell prey to unlikely-sounding fortune-tellers and clairvoyants; he had a strong belief in dreams and in the existence of what he termed his 'spiritual guides'. When he first went to Russia in 1901 he was in correspondence with a Madame Celeste.

His memory of his initial summons to Tsarskoe Selo, some years later, took on a distinctly mystical flavour. He believed he had seen a letter from the palace in a premonition. In an interview he gave in the 1950s, he recalled a series of dizzying details:

I imagined that I'd received [the invitation to work for the Tsar]... It was all sort of mixed up with fantasy and then

I found myself lying half on the floor seeking the letter, because it had slipped from my hands.

The background to Gibbes' summons had in fact been disappointingly prosaic. He was brought in to correct the two elder grand duchesses' accents. The girls' previous tutor, a J. B. M. Epps, had a thick Scots brogue which he had failed to keep out of the classroom.

It was King Edward VII who had first drawn the Tsarina's attention to her daughters' poor vowels. They had addressed him in English during his visit to the Russian Imperial yacht *Standart*. Mr Epps was abruptly handed his cards. Gibbes described his luckless predecessor with wry humour and, perhaps, a touch of condescension. 'He couldn't pronounce "H" at the beginning without an enormous effort which was prominent in all his conversation.'

If, as a Yorkshireman, Gibbes had a regional accent, it was clearly not as strong as that of Mr Epps. None of the people who knew him later in life remembers him having an accent. However his first letters home from St Petersburg read chattily enough: 'It's a funny place, is St Petersburg.'

Having dispatched Epps, the Tsarina instructed a secretary to send an envoy to make inquiries about English teachers at the Consulate. Had she been less of a maverick, she might have acquired an English tutor from one of the Tsar's relations. As it was, she mistrusted the Tsar's relations; she preferred to accept the recommendation of the Consulate. Sydney Gibbes, by then a prominent member of the recently founded Guild of English Teachers, was an obvious choice. She did not feel it necessary to interview him. (Indeed he would work at the palace at Tsarskoe Selo for a full year before he met her.)

Subsequently the Tsarina may well have congratulated herself on her choice. When the crisis came, Gibbes was to demonstrate great bravery, honour and loyalty. However, at the time of the appointment, she seems to have missed pertinent details about his past. Shortly after his arrival in Russia, Gibbes had been effectively dismissed from at least two jobs. He himself never fully understood the circumstances surrounding these departures. The problems probably centred upon his unfathomed emotional life. He harboured a fierce temper which he occasionally failed to control. Though he was rumoured to have been engaged to a suitable Englishwoman, his sexuality remained, apparently, unresolved.

The Tsarina knew none of this. Her information was straightforward: Gibbes combined an excellent academic record with the air of '*un homme comme il faut*'. Within weeks of his summons, Gibbes had taken up the appointment. 'She gave only three directives,' he reported modestly. 'It must be an Englishman, he must have a higher education and be of suitable age.'

He had been born on 19 January 1876, the son of a bank manager. He and his ten siblings grew up in Bank House on Rotherham High Street. They spent their holidays at the family house in Normanton-upon-Trent. No fewer than three of his brothers were to become bank managers: John, the eldest, went to Argentina, William, the second eldest, went to India while the more stolid fourth son, Percy, settled for Gloucester.

As an elderly man, Gibbes spoke very little about his early life. According to one friend, he always believed he should keep his hands to the plough and not look back. However he clearly believed, just as fervently, that he should retain the *possibility* of looking back.

During his life he maintained an apparently comprehensive store of papers collected from the far reaches of Asia and spanning 80 years: press cuttings, bills, menus and travel tickets as well as some intimate journals. Amongst these papers were school reports bristling with plaudits for the young Syd: 'a thoroughly reliable, gentlemanly fellow'. Evidently the bright star of the family, Gibbes studied at University College, Aberystwyth before attending St John's College, Cambridge, where, in 1899, he took his BA (Moral Sciences Tripos). Again, he stored his reports: 'A man of high character, good sense, and agreeable manners'.

At Cambridge Syd added the 'E' to his surname: 'Gibbes', he insisted, was the more historically accurate spelling. He had no compunction about singling himself out from the rest of his family; perhaps he felt some curious obligation to draw attention to his elevated status. One of his friends remembers him evoking, with rueful distaste, the Rotherham air of his childhood days: 'He said he remembered huge clods of smut falling from the sky.'

Following his father's advice, Gibbes took theological courses at Cambridge and Salisbury and attempted to get a curacy. He had already begun to feel, however, that he did not have a true vocation. 'I tried two or three vicars, I didn't like it. I thought it awfully stuffy... I went to the appointments board trying to get a civil job, but I found that was hopeless, nobody wanted a Cambridge graduate in those days.'

Eventually he decided to go to Russia. It was an odd decision: he spoke no Russian and had no connection with Russia. However, the country's very remoteness may have appealed to him. Perhaps he relished the prospect of anonymity and consequent privacy. On a different level he may have been lured by Russia's romantic appeal: he loved the theatre and saw himself as something of a romantic. His tutor at St John's College disapproved of his decision. 'He said, "You won't be anything more than a governess"... Of course it was not at all my job, but I was desperate, I wanted something, so I just took it.'

He spent the summer of 1901 with a family called Shidlovsky. He was taken on as tutor to two boys, aged ten and four. After several days in St Petersburg, he travelled with the family out to their country dacha. He was entranced by the novelty of Russian life, savouring details in letters to his younger sister, Winifred.

> The cabby is always fat. It's an inviolable custom, so if he is not naturally endowed that way… he's obliged to stuff his clothes. No family can have a coachman who is sufficiently thin to be able to walk and the Soborovs [friends of the Shidlovskys] were the proud possessors of one who couldn't lift himself on to his own box seat.

However, in one of his first letters home he described how forcibly it had struck him that Russia was an absolute monarchy. His tone was mildly disapproving. 'If you go to court and have a good position there and have the ear of the Emperor all is well.'

As he travelled through the Russian countryside, he could not have failed to notice the unsettling divide between the rich and poor. In the early 1900s, this divide was so extreme that relations between peasants and landowners were later to be compared to those between African natives and colonial rulers. In his biography of Tolstoy, A. N. Wilson describes Russia's manorial estates and rich houses as islands in an alien sea.

Gibbes was not impressed with his first experience of the Russian Orthodox services. 'The peasants kneel a good deal and make earth bows and touch the ground with the forehead,' he complained. During his first service, a dead baby was brought in, in an open coffin. 'What would people in England think?' He denounced the rituals as 'all rather a jangle'.

Of more immediate concern was his discovery, within the first weeks, that he disliked almost every aspect of his new position. While he marvelled at the Russian landscape – the yellow skies and black earth – he deemed life in the country intolerably dull. He found the constant company of the two small boys unrewarding. The unaccustomed heat oppressed him. At one point hundreds of flies invaded his room and he was obliged to sleep with a handkerchief over his face.

Madame Shidlovsky made efforts to raise his spirits by including him in family entertainment. He noted and acknowledged her efforts, but he must have made a poor companion. On one picnic outing he spent his time totting up the cost: 'One dray, four carriages, one riding horse, 11 other horses, five grooms and three servants for food, 18 labourers to carry a boat across to the water and three women to wash same and bale out the water,' he reported grimly to Winifred.

He yearned for male company. 'Oh *pour un homme*', he sighed in one letter. When he finally met Demie Bebeker, the 15-year-old son of one of the Shidlovskys' neighbours, he was ecstatic. So, it appeared, was Demie. 'There was no shadow of doubt that I was the attraction,' he confessed to Winifred.

Before long, Gibbes decided he wanted to leave the Shidlovskys and work for the Bebekers: 'I thought, as he [Demie] wanted to go to England, they would want somebody and I was pretty well prepared to go for nothing.' He told Winifred that he was willing his 'spiritual guides' to persuade Demie to press their cause upon his mother. Later in the letter he declared himself utterly confounded by Madame Bebeker's rejection of their scheme: '*Je ne pouvais pas comprendre. Il est très étrange,*' he mused in his idiosyncratic French.

He described one incident in which Demie and he had missed their good-night kiss. Social kissing between men was standard practice in Russia at the time. Gibbes gave Winifred two elaborate descriptions of the custom: 'You turn your head very much to the side and you receive a kiss just in front of your ear.' The missed kiss was the cause, evidently, of consternation on both sides. 'I noticed when we said good-night the night before that Demie seemed to think he'd dropped something or missed something, so the next day I mended the error as described.'

Gibbes' happiest period while he was with the Shidlovskys was when the Bebekers came to stay. He reported that he and the two boys all enjoyed frolics with Demie. Unfortunately, Madame Shidlovsky did not approve; Gibbes recognised the disapproval without, apparently, giving any thought to her reasons. Indeed, it is clear from his letters that relations with

'Madame' were increasingly strained. Gibbes seems to have been curiously ham-fisted in his dealings with other people. He was either oblivious or indifferent to their needs. It was a serious flaw in his make-up, rendering him vulnerable and, at times, isolated.

During that first summer in Russia, he was thousands of miles from family and friends, struggling with a strange language. His readiness to alienate those about him borders on the heroic. He was prepared to make life uncomfortable for Madame; he was prepared, apparently, to make his own life intolerable. The most crucial area of conflict between him and Madame centred on his commitment to corporal punishment, a practice Madame deemed barbaric. Recounting the beatings he administered, Gibbes unwittingly portrayed himself as a sort of Wackford Squeers. Was he wedded to Victorian methods of discipline or did he simply lose his temper? He would probably not have examined his motives: his duty was to keep the boys in order. 'I'm a regular Tartar and won't let them have their own way on principle. I don't think they love me much but they will behave,' he told Winifred:

'You must do as you are told. Do you hear?' Spank, spank, spank follows, and a terrific howl... I wouldn't let the elder go into the house, nominally to fetch a book, really to wake his mother. He cried and cried so I just spanked him and he made himself sick and then howled, so I told him he was a pig and could go and lie down in my room till he was better.

In an interview taped in the 1950s he relayed, unabashed, another incident:

He'd got a rake and promised to give me a slosh with it... I said, 'You little devil.' I grabbed him by the scruff of his neck. I put him across my knee and I slapped him as hard as I could. I whacked him, he howled and he'd been eating strawberries and cream and he was sick but I didn't stop, I said 'I'll teach you to use a rake.' But of course he created a terrific din.

This last altercation had taken place while Madame was away. After hearing about it from a horrified nanny, Madame became reluctant to leave Gibbes alone with the boys. He saw this as nothing more than an inconvenience: 'Madame is so awfully nervous and frightened if the children are out of her sight. It's awfully tiresome.' In fact, he was rather proud of his progress with his terrified charges who were, he assured Winifred, increasingly like 'cherubs'.

The crisis in his relations with Madame came when, over one dinner in July, he was asked by a fellow diner to give his opinion of one of the boys. His self-restraint failed him and he found himself embroiled in one of his lone offensives:

> Perhaps rather foolishly I told them. I dressed him down and so on. Then the mother flared up and we had a set-to right there... I showed her what she was doing and what I was doing and I gave my opinion that she was doing harm. I don't think she will interfere much now but I am quite sure she just hates me.

He and Madame argued till 12.30. 'I begin to think I've got an awful tongue when it's set going,' he added to Winifred, with apparent remorse.

> She had difficulty to prevent tears at times... The criticism of my work was in such wise that I had succeeded in gain-

ing a moral ascendancy over the boy and done him much good… but I had failed in small things. I did not see that he washed his hands properly and didn't get his toes wet.

It is hard to gauge Winifred's reactions to these disquieting reports. There was seldom any reference to her in his letters. He was, however, driven to devote a great deal of space to her after she had sent him a miniature portrait of herself: 'I don't very much like it,' he began starkly. He drew diagrams demonstrating its flawed rendering of her shoulders and told her that her hair had not taken nicely. Lastly he added that one of the boys had thought she looked 41 (she was 20).

He habitually signed his letters to her 'your loving brother Charles' rather than just 'Syd'. Occasionally he went further and signed himself 'Karl Ivanovich'. These flourishes were probably less shared jokes than a sort of fanciful posturing. As a doting younger sister, Winifred would have been an eager and uncritical recipient of everything her brother cared to offer.

In August Madame decided to send Gibbes back to St Petersburg a full month early. Gibbes read nothing into her decision. 'She said that she would have the house full of visitors and she thought perhaps it wouldn't interest me very much and perhaps I would like to be released,' he recalled breezily.

Misfortune seemed to dog him. Shortly after his return to St Petersburg, he was asked to leave his apartment. His landlady dismissed him with the strange indictment: 'You live very quiet, you live very quiet, but you disturb my guests.' It is hard to imagine which of Gibbes' quiet habits so disturbed her guests, but the landlady was evidently prepared to forfeit her rent in order to be rid of him. In the 1950s interview he relayed all this with robust cheer, tutting genially over the foibles of landladies: 'There's nowt so queer as folk.'

According to one source, he then worked for a family called Soukanoff and in 1902 brought his pupil to England. The pair returned in high spirits and loaded with presents. However, soon after their return, Gibbes learnt that the Soukanoffs did not wish to re-employ him. He was never offered a reason for the dismissal.

Worn with a certain dash, misfortune can be an

attractive asset; Gibbes probably wore his rather heavily. Nonetheless, he had a responsive help-mate – a P. Otten, with effeminate writing – who saw him through his misadventures. Gibbes relished formal relationships: he had several correspondents with whom he exchanged decorous confidences. This restrained mode of communication would have been preferable, in his view, to the more robust intimacy of a chat in the pub.

'Remember our disappointments are God's appointments,' P. Otten assured him obscurely in April. 'I don't believe you would have been happy with the Soukanoffs. They are not particularly nice people and the boy is very slow, Mrs Webb says.' In September there were further commiserations over his mother and sister's visit to St Petersburg. 'I feel very sorry for you. I did hope you were going to have a nice time with your sister and you say you spent most of your time alone in your lodgings.'

He had at least one further falling-out with an unco-operative mother. He accompanied a Russian family to Germany. According to Gibbes, the son was, once again, spoilt and overindulged. On one occasion, the mother bought her son a succession of three walking sticks. 'We went to the zoo. We went to the monkeys and the monkeys were hopping about. Then the stick was in the cage… Gone.' The next one was lost during a carriage ride. The boy was waving it about, insisting he drive; he dropped it under the carriage wheels. The third stick was lost on a mushroom-picking expedition. The mother's profligacy and lack of any sense of discipline proved too much for Gibbes: 'When they said "We're going to the country," I said, "You must excuse me but I cannot, I just cannot," and so they just let me go.'

Over the next six years Gibbes divided his time between Russia and England. He would teach in St Petersburg for six months of the year and spend the other six months in Yorkshire. He felt the existence was vacuous and was plagued by self-doubt. 'I used to scold myself. I used to say you mustn't go on like this, you must do something.'

However, by 1907 he had qualified as vice-president and committee member of the St Petersburg Guild of English Teachers. The aim of the guild was 'to brighten the lives of the governesses or teachers by means of occasional social gatherings'. Gibbes brightened the lives of his fellow teachers with his acting. When Winifred returned to St Petersburg with him in the summer of 1907, the pair became a sort of comic duo. Amongst Gibbes' papers are playbills on which 'Mr Gibbes and Miss Gibbes' feature prominently. Highlights included the sketch 'A Pair of Lunatics' and readings from 'The Obstructive Hat'.

In 1911 a Miss Cade is billed under 'Extras: "Only Me" by Miss Cade'. Little is known about Laura Anna Cade except that she was a resident of St Petersburg and was clearly well acquainted with Gibbes. They were even rumoured to have been engaged; in 1916 they joined forces to buy Pritchard's English School for Modern Languages. However, when Gibbes followed the Imperial family to Siberia, he dissolved the partnership. There seems to be only one subsequent reference to Miss Cade in Gibbes' correspondence. In December 1917 his former servant Katya wrote simply 'Miss Cade is in good health.'

The extent of Gibbes' emotional involvement with Miss Cade cannot be known; his commitment to the courtship may have been born simply of his passion for doing the right thing. However, she seems to have made a strong impression upon his unconscious. There were several references to 'Miss C' in a dream diary Gibbes kept while courting her. She emerges as something of a killjoy. In one dream Gibbes is attending a fête while a band is being conducted by a man with a cockerel mask. 'The song was very funny and everybody was enjoying it very much when suddenly Miss C. ran in and said: "Oh, come and see father's better rabbit," which was very absurd.'

At one point Gibbes taught at a girls' finishing school. But when he received his letter from the Imperial family he was working as an usher at the Imperial School of Law, attended only by sons of the hereditary nobility. He thought the school shoddy and hated the job:

Nicholas Nickleby was an usher... it's a terrible position... They had a system which I'd never seen in any other school. They had a certain number of overcoats hanging up in the cloakroom and you went and selected your coat, just took the first one that came... consequently nobody cared about these clothes, they were picked to pieces... they [the boys] looked most awful ragamuffins.'

***

It was in the autumn of 1908 that Gibbes made his first appearance at the palace. He wore traditional evening dress, as was the custom even during the day. The incongruity of his outfit made him uncomfortable: 'The etiquette was that persons who had not a uniform wore evening dress... I set off to the Palace in evening dress at 6.00 in the morning. A ghastly experience.'

Initially, Gibbes was obliged to fit his Imperial appointment in with various other jobs. Twice a week he would travel the 15 miles from St Petersburg to Tsarskoe Selo on the train; from the station he would take a drozhky to the palace.

When he first took up his appointment, Grand Duchess Olga was 13, Tatiana 11, Marie nine, Anastasia seven and the Tsarevich Alexis four. The Imperial children did not have a good reputation.

According to Princess Elizabeth Naryhshkin they 'generally behaved like young savages'. Later, as young women, the grand duchesses apparently spoke like ten-year-old girls, giggling, poking each other and running into corners. Gibbes saw none of this. Indeed he later paid tribute to the girls' decorum in making no comment when he – to his horror – forgot to put his tie on.

I took as my first lesson the two elder girls. They took their lessons together. Olga and Tatiana... Then I had the third daughter by herself, and the third daughter was the most charming of all, the sweetest character and the greatest of them in artistic talent.

While he was teaching the older girls, the young Tsarevich would visit the schoolroom. Gibbes was immediately captivated by him.

A tiny little chap in wee wee white knickerbockers and a Russian shirt trimmed with Ukrainian embroidery of blue and silver. He used to toddle into my class room at 11 o'clock, look around and then gravely shake hands.

A year later, however, Gibbes' schoolroom idyll came to an abrupt end with the arrival of the Grand Duchess Anastasia. Anastasia was remembered by surviving cousins as a mischievous little girl, wild and rough, a hair-puller and tripper-up of servants. Gibbes acknowledged her shortcomings with characteristic restraint: 'The little Grand Duchess was not always an easy child to instruct… We had, as a rule, charming lessons, but sometimes there were storms.'

Once she tried to bribe Gibbes, offering him a bunch of flowers in return for his raising her mark. Another time, the morning after a children's fancy dress ball, she came into the classroom with her face blackened like a chimney-sweep and carrying a small ladder. Gibbes decided to ignore her and carry on with the lesson. The Tsarina, however, came in a few minutes later. She was furious with her daughter: 'Anastasia, go and change at once.' Gibbes was to recall that morning to good effect when, some 40 years later, he finally confronted the best-known 'false' Anastasia, Anna Anderson.

Though he had made such a delightful first impression upon Gibbes, the young Tsarevich also

Gibbes with Anastasia in the schoolroom

proved a troublesome pupil. Gibbes began teaching the nine-year-old Tsarevich in 1913. At first the boy seemed to be in the thrall of his tutor. 'Was most observant of ME and my clothes and actions,' he wrote wryly in his diary. Unfortunately, Alexis' fascination did not last; he was soon in search of fresh stimuli. 'In the middle of the hour he asked permission to ring for Derevenko [his sailor servant] whom he asked for sweets,' Gibbes wrote. 'The sailor returned bringing a chocolate in a glass which the infant ate with relish. The habit has begun and ought to be stopped. It is piggish to eat like that in company.'

Despite the course in child psychology he had attended at Cambridge, Gibbes had great difficulty controlling Alexis. At one point they made paper hats together. This proved such a success that Alexis couldn't be prevented from making more and more hats. Another time the Tsarevich brought in wire and he and Gibbes made telephones. The idea was to hold the wire to the ear and between the teeth. This project also disintegrated into a skirmish as the Tsarevich struggled to fasten wire to Gibbes' teeth against his wishes. A third battle involved Alexis running about the room brandishing scissors; the more Gibbes remonstrated with him, the more he shrieked and laughed. Gibbes noted, with disapproval, a change in the Tsarevich's appearance on these occasions. 'He doesn't look handsome then: a most curious expression.' At that time Gibbes had no idea the Tsarevich was a haemophiliac. Had he known, he would have been considerably more disturbed by the boy's antics. The Tsarevich's illness was being kept secret, evidently even from his tutors.

Gibbes was not the only adult to fall victim to Alexis' wilfulness. The boy once ordered a band of sentries to march out to sea on foot. The Tsar used to joke that he trembled for Russia under 'Alexei the Terrible'. Gibbes later recalled arguments as he tried to persuade the boy to wear a thick coat; eventually the Tsar himself would be obliged to set an example by putting on his own thick coat: 'Naturally he could not refuse to follow when Papa led.' The Tsarina was widely acknowledged as too soft with her son. But the criticism Gibbes expresses towards her is remarkably mild, bearing little resemblance to the scathing judgments he cast upon the mothers of his lesser-born charges. 'His mother was perhaps more amenable to persuasion and might sometimes, though not often, be induced to change the parental laws which governed his little life.'

With his Imperial appointment, Gibbes' mild hauteur had found its element: he clearly relished the formality and propriety of palace life. He had finally found what he deemed a worthwhile focus for his energies, and from 1908 to 1917 he must have been extremely content. He would have been gratified by the reflection that he had come a long way from his uncomfortable summer with the Shidlovskys; and a still longer way from his childhood days in the busy 'quiverful' atmosphere of Bank House, Rotherham.

Gibbes out riding with the Tsarevich

He was ready to look uncritically, even kindly, on most of those around him. The Tsar and Tsarina were particular favourites. He recognised, and revelled in, their charm. They, in turn, would presumably have appreciated the devotion of a pleasant and cultured English gentleman.

The Tsar was generally considered rather a colourless character. His father, Alexander III, had walked through doors without opening them and twisted forks in knots by way of a party trick. But Gibbes was quite satisfied with the current Tsar's quieter attributes:

He had a presence that was second to none, so full of quiet and assured self-possession and dignity. But it never inspired fear... I think that the reason for this was his eyes. Yes, I am sure that it was his eyes, so wonderful were they. Of the most delicate shade of blue, that looked you straight in the face with the kindest, the tenderest, the most loving expression.'

The Tsarina was a formidable woman who was alluded to as 'The Colonel' in certain salons. She once famously declared that 'Russia likes to feel the whip.' According to Lili Dehn, the wife of one of the Tsar's naval commanders and a close friend, the Tsarina liked to play games but displayed a 'lovable weakness... She never liked to lose.' While Gibbes was discomforted by her regular appearances during lessons, he was thrilled by the way she wielded her power. 'Not haughty in the ordinary sense, she never forgot her position,' he enthused, 'she looked queenly, but I was always at ease with her... she had a fresh complexion and beautiful hair and eyes. She gave you her hand with dignity mingled with shyness, which gave her a truly gracious air.' Later he felt compelled, in the interest of veracity, to add that her feet were large.

He recognised the Tsarina's fatal lack of popularity amongst her subjects:

I think that the cause of this must be attributed to the Empress's lack of a theatrical sense. The theatrical instinct is so deeply engrained in the Russian nature that one often feels that Russians act their lives rather than live them. This was completely foreign to the Empress's school of thought... which she had mostly acquired under the tutelage of her revered grandmother Queen Victoria.

The Tsarina had a number of English tastes: she loved chintz and had her furniture mail-ordered from Maples. Gibbes was slightly disapproving: 'I didn't care much for the style you know, but of course everything was done in a subdued and good tone so it was not unpleasant.' She was indifferent to the quality of food. Gibbes reported that she was prone to eat chicken cutlets twice daily for months on end. 'The Empress herself was more than abstemious and had small appreciation of the pleasures of good living. The food of the Palace was often atrocious as a direct consequence of this.'

With regard to the spiritual side of the Tsarina's life, many memoirs of life at the pre-revolutionary Russian court focus on her involvement with the peasant 'holy man' Rasputin. Her reverence for the rake who exposed himself in a St Petersburg nightclub has been deemed a factor in the collapse of the monarchy. Few of her critics at the time knew that her attachment was founded on her poignant belief that he could heal her son.

Unfortunately the Tsarina's faith in Rasputin's divine powers grew to the point where she felt he must extend his dominion. If he could heal Alexis, why should he not solve the ills of the country? At one point, she was even advising the Tsar to part his hair with Rasputin's comb before important political meetings.

The growing influence of the 'holy man' was viewed with dismay, particularly amongst the Russian aristocracy; blame for the failing popularity of the Imperial family was laid firmly at his door. In December 1916 he was poisoned and shot by Prince Felix Yussoupov and Grand Duke Dmitri, before drowning in the Neva. Yussoupov apparently kept one of the bullets and wore it in a ring on his finger.

Gilliard once sighted the 'holy man' in an anteroom. He made much of the moment: 'I had the distinct impression that I was in the presence of a sinister and evil being.' Gibbes, however, for all his relish of drama, resisted any temptation to overplay his memory of Rasputin. This may have been out of loyalty to the Tsarina. Or he may simply have remained unimpressed. After more than ten years in Russia, he had probably grown accustomed to the controversial appearance and habits of the '*stranniki*' (pilgrims) who roamed the countryside. More importantly, he was not convinced that Rasputin had ever wielded power at the court. One of Gibbes' friends, the former British ambassador David Beattie, kept a record of a conversation with Gibbes in 1961: 'He [Gibbes] didn't consider Rasputin influential or harmful; he was simply a peasant with naïve cunning and some healing powers.'

Gibbes told another friend, Dmitri Kornhardt, that he had encountered Rasputin only once. Dmitri pressed him for details, alluding to his filthy appearance. Gibbes would only reply enigmatically: 'Rasputin did not have the odour of the great unwashed.'

The historian George Katkov recalls Gibbes telling him that he once saw the Tsar throw a letter from one of Rasputin's detractors straight into the wastepaper basket. Gibbes had brought the Tsarevich to the Tsar's military headquarters at Mogilev. Gibbes recalled the Tsar's irritation: 'Another of those denunciations of Gregory. I get them almost every day and throw them away unread.'

When war broke out in 1914, Gibbes was in England on holiday with his father in Normanton. John Gibbs had recovered from his disappointment at his son's rejection of the church. Indeed, he had written rapturously when he heard of his son's Imperial appointment: 'If only your dear mother had lived to see this.' Mary Gibbs had died in 1906. It was the last time father and son would be together. John Gibbs was to die in April 1917.

Gibbes received a telegram ordering him back to Russia. When he reached the palace, he found the flavour of life changed.

> For one thing, they [our lives] were very much fuller, everybody was frantically busy. The Emperor's official duties increased enormously, he never seemed to have any free time. Even the hours when he took his exercise in the park were often cut into – an unheard-of thing. The Empress was busy all day long with her Red Cross work and with her correspondence.

The Tsarina ended up taking Veronal to ease the strain. 'Veronal is keeping me up. I'm literally saturated with it,' she proclaimed to Lili Dehn.

Inspired by news of the war, the Tsarevich insisted on changing his costume. 'He ceased to wear his sailor's uniform, which hitherto had been his invariable attire. He now wore the uniform of a simple soldier, with a miniature rifle to match, accurately made to scale,' reported Gibbes.

Increasingly in demand, Gibbes agreed to take up residence at Tsarskoe Selo. He kept his flat in St Petersburg, but was obliged to give up most of his work in the city. Over the last six years he had managed to fit extra English classes around his Imperial appointment; he was now the director of several Higher Courses at the Pritchard English School for Modern Languages. 'In compensation the Empress very kindly gave me a nice little flat in the

The Alexander Palace, Tsarskoe Selo, in which the Romanovs lived; Gibbes stayed in the Catherine Palace nearby.

magnificent Palace of Catherine II,' he wrote.

Gibbes was able to take the Tsarevich for walks around the palace and its grounds. On one occasion they came upon two men smashing crockery. If crockery intended for the Imperial family was found to be damaged, it had to be destroyed. Nobody else was allowed to use it.

It was probably at this time that Gibbes began his dream diary, perhaps as a way of passing his free evenings. He was to fill 27 pages with records of dreams spanning just two months. He wrote three headings across the top of each page: 'Date', 'Dreams' and 'Remarks', each heading underlined twice in red ink. The 'Remarks' section remained blank and was dropped after two pages. Among the more bizarre dreams is one in which he whips up a horse in order to jump a barrier; the horse turns into a lean bear. Another involves a prospective pupil who 'had at the neck a long brooch composed of a single row of diamonds and diamonds on his teeth.'

Social insecurity is a recurring theme. In one dream Gilliard is presenting himself to the Tsar and has forgotten his decoration; the decoration is lying on a table behind the Tsar and Gilliard reaches clumsily over the Tsar to retrieve it. The Tsar is furious but Gilliard just sits down on an easy chair and laughs. Gibbes reflects on his discomfort: 'I felt it was exceedingly out of place to laugh and didn't do so. I felt I didn't know what to do.'

In July 1916 Gibbes began a commonplace book. He described the beauty of the gardens of Tsarskoe Selo. He claimed to regret the proximity of Tsarskoe Selo to St Petersburg, but confessed 'I... oft journey thither.'

He 'journeyed thither' twice in order to visit a fortune-teller, Dyadya (Uncle) Misha Konnaya. Konnaya's grasp of the future may have been sound but his grasp of the past was poor. Though there were barely three weeks between Gibbes' two visits, the fortune-teller made it clear during the second session that he had no recollection of the first. Noting the lapse, Gibbes was unfazed; he recorded in detail Konnaya's every word: 'You can only be a scientist, a pastor, a doctor, a pedagogue, an artist, a musician or a lawyer. On no account go into commerce, it will always be a failure.' Konnaya did not rate Gibbes' chances of marrying. Recording Konnaya's words, Gibbes may have spared a thought for the unfortunate Miss Cade: 'You are of a type that generally never marries but if marriage does take place let it be an intellectual union, not a union for the sake of face or fortune...' Lastly, Konnaya predicted a journey: 'It will take place in the second half of July or the first days of August.' Gibbes added a postscript: 'NB on the first occasion he said that it would be in July.'

On 4 August Gibbes did indeed receive a telephone call from Gilliard, giving him details of a trip he was to make. Gibbes was to accompany the Tsarevich to the military headquarters at Mogilev. The Tsar was anxious to have his son with him at Mogilev; he was equally anxious that Alexis should continue his English lessons.

Gibbes stayed at the Hotel France and every morning made his way up the hill to the Governor's House, where the Tsar and the Tsarevich were staying. 'The teaching staff was a very small one, consisting of two or three persons only,' he wrote, 'but it was all very friendly and gay and, according to the Tsarevich, infinitely preferable to Tsarskoe Selo.'

The Tsar insisted that Gibbes and Alexis sit in his 'cabinet' while he worked. 'Once', Gibbes recalled, 'he overheard the Tsarevich telling me that... he was going to take the big cut-glass ball that hung on the electric chandelier. "Alexei!" the Emperor shouted out. "That isn't ours."' After the Tsarevich had gone to bed, the Tsar would come and say prayers with him. 'While we were waiting for his coming we would read or talk or sometimes amuse ourselves with the cat.'

Later that year Gibbes made the curious decision to keep a diary written from Alexis' point of view. It is tempting to draw sinister inferences: Gibbes had an unwholesome yearning to become part of Alexis, or even to *be* Alexis. In fact, he may well have adopted the new stance in the same spirit of slightly grim play-acting with which he had signed himself 'Karl Ivanovich'. He now referred to himself as 'C. S. G':

8 October:... Lessons as usual... after lunch motored to the wood on the Orshansky Road where we played at robbers...

Thursday 13 October: Came home not feeling very well, by the doctor's orders went to bed at 6.30 pm. Very poorly all evening, stomach quite upset. C.S.G. read, but with difficulty could pay any attention...

By December, Alexis was so ill that it was decided he should return to Tsarskoe Selo. Gibbes still did not know that the Tsarevich had haemophilia; he was probably told when he joined the Imperial family in exile. He does not seem to have dwelt upon the nature of the Tsarevich's illness, but then he probably never saw him seriously ill. Perhaps more surprising, even with his mellower outlook, was his lack of concern over the missed lessons.

During February four of the five Imperial children became ill with measles. The Tsarina gave Gibbes quarters in the Alexander Palace so that he could be on call at all hours. She felt it worth noting that, when summoned late to read to Alexis, 'Sig' – the family's nickname for Gibbes – would appear in his dressing-gown.

Towards the end of February, events in St Petersburg spun out of control. Opposition had been growing to Russia's involvement in the war; widespread discontent with the autocracy of Tsarist rule, simmering for decades, now bubbled to the surface. The hard-pressed people were ready to rally in the spirit of Marx's dark assurance: 'The proletarians have nothing to lose but their chains.'

Rumours of impending bread shortages triggered a panic reaction on the streets. Within 24 hours textile workers had gone on strike; they were joined by tens of thousands more strikers who then all took to the streets. The police, on orders from the Duma, took no action. Soldiers brought in to quell the disturbances simply joined the strikers. Gibbes, absorbed in the decorum of life at Tsarskoe Selo, was slow to grasp the gravity of the situation. Perhaps this is hardly surprising: the Tsar himself fought shy of the facts. In January the British ambassador, Sir George Buchanan, had issued him with a stark warning: 'If I were to see a friend walking through a wood on a dark night along a path which I knew ended in a precipice would it not be my duty, sir, to warn him of the danger?' Though shaken, the Tsar failed to act sufficiently decisively.

By 28 February, the city was at a virtual standstill and, in desperation, the ministers cabled the Tsar, who had now returned to the front. Members of the State Council sent a telegram: '...The government, never having enjoyed Russia's trust, is utterly discredited and completely powerless to deal with the grave situation... Further delays and vacillations threaten untold misfortunes.'

On March 2 1917 the Tsar abdicated, bringing to an end 300 years of Romanov rule. At first he abdicated in favour of his son, then in favour of his brother, Grand Duke Michael. Within 24 hours Grand Duke Michael, too, had rejected the throne.

At Tsarskoe Selo, Gibbes' increasingly important role was to divert Alexis. His diary reverted to his own point of view. He now began double-dating his entries. Up until the revolution, the Russians had subscribed to the Julian calendar. Now they adopted the Gregorian calendar, 13 days ahead:

Thursday 2/15 March: Patient better and able to play. Constructed model houses and read aloud. Day passed much as usual. Everybody anxious about the issue of events. No trains to Petrograd since morning.

During the evening of the following day, the Tsar's uncle, Grand Duke Paul, arrived at Tsarskoe Selo to inform the Tsarina that the Tsar had abdicated. She had been reluctant to accept the rumours of revolution: 'The peasants love us,' she insisted to Lili Dehn. She decided she would not tell the children immediately. Life in the nursery remained tranquil:

Saturday 4/17 March: [Tsarevich] better but not in very good spirits. Knows nothing of passing events, but feels them all the same. We cast lead bullets and built model houses.

On Sunday the Empress gave orders for a 'Te Deum' to be sung. The miraculous icon from one of the churches at Tsarskoe Selo was brought to the palace and taken through the children's sickrooms. The procession, including the Tsarina, passed through the deserted rooms of the palace. Gibbes made no reference to the service. He did mention the cutting off of the palace water supply, but only in passing:

5/18 March: Patient not quite so well. [We stayed] In the classroom as there being no water it was not possible to heat the playroom hot-water pipes.

The following Friday the Tsarina persuaded Gibbes to take a day off. He called into his flat in St Petersburg and then visited the language school. While he was absent, the Tsarina was informed that she was under arrest. The few members of the household who wanted to stay in the palace were told they were also under arrest.

Upon his return, Gibbes was alarmed to find himself locked out. He immediately appealed to Sir George Buchanan for help. While awaiting a response, he made himself useful as a sort of courier for the captive family. He based himself in his rooms at the Catherine Palace. A servant would collect his meals from the Imperial kitchen and in this way he kept abreast of the worsening conditions inside. He was greatly distressed to hear that Alexis' sailor assistant, Derevenko, had reversed roles with the Tsarevich; Alexis was now being ordered about by the assistant. Another of the Tsarina's captive coterie,

Anna Vyrubova, reported that Alexis obeyed the sailor's savage commands 'in dazed confusion'.

The palace had by this time neither water nor light. 'No longer was there the coming and going of the outside world – the pulse of life had stopped,' wrote Gibbes. After a long delay, his letter requesting admission to the palace came back with a refusal. This refusal, he recalled with bleak satisfaction, was endorsed by no less than five ministers of the Provisional government.

Months later, the Tsar told Gibbes that when the Provisional Leader, Kerensky, finally summoned the courage to visit the family, he was very nervous. He kept bending a paper-knife until the Tsar, fearful that it would snap, took it away.

As the revolution raged around him, Gibbes found his somewhat neglected republican tendencies in conflict with his personal predicament. In a letter to his Uncle Will, then editor of the *Sheffield Daily Chronicle*, he expressed his divided feelings: 'Our world is upside down. In most things the change is for the better, although personally the opposite is the case.'

Still underestimating the seriousness of the up-heavals, Gibbes was contemplating a new business venture. In the teeth of Konnaya's advice, he suggested to Uncle Will that he market an efficient kitchen stove in Russia: the Barnsley Smokeless Cooker. Was he proposing to combine marketing stoves with teaching the Imperial children? Whatever the case, his request was urgent: 'Can you send me as early as possible particulars of the Barnsley Smokeless Fuel Company Ltd?'

That same month Gibbes received news from his Aunt Hattie of his father's death. He had not seen his father for three years; it is impossible to gauge how much the news upset him. In his reply he talked little of his own sorrow. He did tell Aunt Hattie that he would send a list, the following day, of items belonging to his father that he now wanted. He believed he would soon be returning to England for good. '...It is more than possible that I shall leave Russia and return to England with my "pupil",' he wrote. He added something of an apology for his precipitate request. 'It is only the distance and time that it takes to communicate that emboldens me to send you the list straight off in the first place.'

There was indeed a period of several weeks when the family could have come to England. On 22 March a telegram was received from George V offering the family asylum; they were to travel to the North of Russia, to be met by a British cruiser. However, the Tsarina had been reluctant to move the children while they were ill; no one had appreciated the urgency of their situation. Then, in the summer, the British government withdrew the invitation. It was believed by the Russians at the time that it was the British Prime Minister, Lloyd George, who persuaded George V to go back on his offer. It is now known that it was the King himself who made the decision. He apparently feared that the presence of the Imperial family would embarrass the Crown and irritate Labour MPs. An additional factor may have been the family's supposed pro-German tendencies.

***

In August 1917 Gibbes finally received permission to join the family in their exile in Tobolsk, Siberia. He attempted to leave straightaway but was delayed by a train strike. When he finally left, he took with him an enormous amount of books. He wrote later that he expected to be put into prison and intended to while away his solitary hours with John Richard Green's *A Short History of the English People*. In the end it was the Tsar who read it in Tobolsk. 'I very much wanted him to write an appreciation on the fly leaf but I was too shy to [ask him to] do so.'

The journey to Tobolsk from St Petersburg was long and uncomfortable. The Tsarina's lady-in-waiting, Baroness Sophie Buxhoeveden, who made the same journey at roughly the same time, found her train so crowded that she was obliged to travel part of the way on the carriage roof.

Gibbes caught the last river-boat from Tiumen to Tobolsk before the seven-month Siberian winter set in. He arrived at Tobolsk in early October. Upon arrival he approached the commissar put in charge of the family by the Provisional Government, Vasily Pankratov; Pankratov allotted him a room in a house just opposite the Governor's House, where the Imperial family was confined:

Permission to enter Government House was not immediately granted. Apparently the case had to be submitted to the soldiers. But the next day I was informed that no objection had been raised. This was a greater privilege than I then realised, for none of those who came to Tobolsk afterwards was ever admitted.

Gibbes was well received by the Tsarina, from whom he had been separated for seven months. 'The Empress was sitting at table with the Tsarevich and received me with every sign of pleasure after my long enforced absence. She was particularly happy to receive news of her friends.' Gibbes had visited Anna Vyrubova before leaving St Petersburg. He had taken a photograph of her at the Tsarina's request. Anna Vyrubova had been taken from the palace and imprisoned by Provisional Government guards after the family was placed under arrest; she had been treated brutally. The Tsarina evidently felt she could somehow share her friend's suffering by poring over the photographic evidence.

Gibbes' reunion with the Tsar was a mixed affair. 'He absolutely pounced on me at first, for it was from English sources that he had received the severest blows. Attacks from revolutionary leaders in Russia he knew he must take and suffer, but those from England – to which he had been so loyal – had to be the unkindest cut of all,' he recalled.

The Tsar was hurt by the British Government's withdrawal of its offer of an exile for the family. But at court there was also a prevalent belief – outlined in Anna Vyrubova's memoirs – that the British themselves were in some part behind the revolution. Vyrubova accuses the British Ambassador Sir George Buchanan of colluding with Tsar Nicholas' hostile Grand Duke cousins.

Gibbes resumed classes with the children in Tobolsk. Lessons began at nine, but were broken off from 11 to 12 for a walk. Lunch was at one o'clock. After lunch Gibbes or Gilliard read to the Tsarevich. After tea lessons went on until 6.30. Dinner was one hour later.

Anastasia reclaimed her role as Gibbes' most troublesome pupil. One day, when she was particularly boisterous, he snapped at her; she promptly added his expostulation to the name on the front of her book and, from then on, referred to herself as: 'Shut up'.

Pankratov observed the pupils at their lessons; he was not impressed by the teaching staff. 'With the exception of the Frenchman Gilliard and the English-man Gibbes, the rest were just courtiers,' he wrote. He reported the comments of a teacher he himself brought in to teach the children. 'They had read little Pushkin, even less Lermontov and have never even heard of Nekrasov... Alexis has a hazy concept of Russian geography. What does this mean?'

In November 1917 the Bolshevik party seized power from Kerensky and his Provisional Government. Within a few months, Lenin had trans-ferred the Russian capital from St Petersburg to Moscow and begun sowing the seeds of the 'Red Terror'.

News of the coup d'état arrived in Tobolsk several weeks later, contained in a bundle of old newspapers. The Tsar was in despair. 'The Emperor abdicated because he thought it would be better for Russia. It turned out to be worse. He did not expect this, and he suffered dreadful remorse on account of his action,' wrote Gibbes. Further strictures were introduced.

'We were given a soldier's ration and ordered to limit our necessities to 150 roubles per week… we began to get inferior food. Only two courses of soup and meat were now served.'

One of the guards, Colonel Yevgeny Kobylinsky, recorded that Government money had run out. The Tsar's cook, Khariotonov, complained he was no longer trusted in the shops. At a loss, Kobylinsky went to see the director of the Tobolsk branch of the National Bank. The director advised him to approach a monarchist who had a large amount of money in the bank; the merchant agreed to grant Kobylinsky a loan of 20,000 roubles.

Gibbes later referred plaintively to his time at Tobolsk as 'unfortunate yet somehow happy'. He must have relished his intimacy with the family, but, within a month of his arrival, his stress was sufficiently evident to have caught the attention of Gilliard. Gilliard made what sounded like a wry reference to Gibbes in a letter to the tutors' colleague, the Russian teacher Petrov. 'The anxiety that has pursued you for weeks wears on the nervous system. Gibbes himself feels the effects of it, despite his

British imperturbability.' Gibbes' own recollections of Tobolsk focus on the frustrations of his employers. 'The Emperor found it harder to fill up his leisure time. During his hours of exercise he would walk up and down the yard 40 or 50 times an hour and when that proved too monotonous he would saw some logs.'

In December Gibbes wrote a letter to the Tsarina's former English governess, Miss Margaret Jackson, apparently at the behest of the Tsarina, who had corresponded with 'Madgie' regularly over the years. His detailed descriptions of the location of the house and lay-out of its interior were obviously intended for use in some rescue attempt. He had never written to her before.

> Our House or rather Houses, for there are two… are the best in town. That in which the Household proper lives is entirely isolated and possesses a small garden beside a piece of the roadway which has been railed in to make a recreation ground…

The letter contained a passing reference to the

Prince of Wales; it was clearly meant to be shown to King George V.

Throughout his time in Tobolsk, Gibbes was impressed by the strong religious faith of the family, particularly that of the Tsarina. However, he was at pains to stress that her adherence to religion 'was not the product of hysteria' as was subsequently claimed. He recalled that they were at first allowed to go every Sunday to the early service at the parish church in Tobolsk. Unfortunately the priest, Father Vasiliev, failed to exclude the traditional blessing for the Imperial family. The Red Guards present were horrified and the family was forbidden from going to church in the town again. 'Instead of this a special chaplain was appointed... henceforward we had our services in an improvised church in the house.'

Christmas was a doleful affair. The Tsarina was apparently the only one who maintained a semblance of high spirits. She presented a Gospel to each of the soldiers, with a hand-painted bookmark. She made presents for some of the servants and for Gibbes she copied a prayer. Much was made of her thoughtfulness in providing the soldiers and Dr Botkin's family with a Christmas tree. Unfortunately Gleb Botkin later recalled that the effect of the tree was to lower rather than raise the spirits: it had no decorations.

In January, Gibbes and Gilliard had the idea of raising morale by staging amateur Sunday evening theatricals, made up of one-act plays in French, English and Russian. On 17 February, Gibbes directed an English play entitled 'Packing Up' – a light farce by Harry Grattan – in which Anastasia created an unexpected sensation. 'They were getting through the "business" so fast that a draught got under the gown and whisked its tail up to the middle of her back, showing her sturdy legs and bottom encased in the Emperor's Jaeger underwear,' recalled Gibbes. 'We all gasped. Emperor and Empress, suite and servants, collapsed in uncontrolled laughter... it was the last heartily unrestrained laughter the Empress ever enjoyed.' This last comment has a slightly theatrical ring to it: Gibbes was not with the Tsarina for the last three months of her life.

In March, the Bolshevik government signed a peace treaty with the Germans at Brest-Litovsk, surrendering about a third of Russia's eastern territory.

The Tsarina, wrongly labelled a German sympathiser, was particularly distraught. She declared that she could not think about Brest-Litovsk without a pain in her heart. 'All one's feelings have been trampled underfoot,' she lamented.

Restrictions tightened once more on the family. The Tsar was ordered to remove his epaulettes. It was now decided that the retinue should be cut in half and that the remaining retainers, with the exception of the doctors, be sent to live with the Imperial family in the Governor's Mansion. Gibbes' options were referred to at a meeting of the Soviet Presidium to discuss 'the guarding of Nicholas in Tobolsk'. It was resolved 'to offer the English language teacher a choice of either living with the arrested or ceasing all relations with them'.

When he heard of the new strictures, Gibbes created some merriment among the grand duchesses by flatly refusing to move in with Gilliard. Though they had worked together at the Russian court for nine years, there was little love lost between the two tutors. Later, in 1921, Gibbes would condemn Gilliard for writing his memoirs; Gilliard, in his turn, mentioned

Gibbes just twice in 300 pages, and that simply in passing. Still, throughout the 1920s, the two would maintain a friendly front, exchanging letters dominated by complaints about ill health. Incidentally, both men lived on into their eighties.

The magnificent Russian court was now reduced to a few retainers held captive in Siberia. The extraordinary nature of the situation could not have escaped Gibbes. But to what extent he was upset and to what extent simply intrigued cannot be known. His awkward temperament certainly became increasingly evident. Dr Botkin's children later referred to him as a 'pig-headed Englishman'. He was eventually allowed to lodge alone with his servant, Anfisa, in a lean-to next to the kitchen. 'He won't live anywhere without Fisa,' giggled the grand duchesses. This probably would have had less to do with Fisa's personal attractions than her domestic skills: Gibbes set great store by personal hygiene.

On 9 April 1918 a new commissar, Vasily Yakovlev, arrived at Tobolsk and informed the Tsar that the family had to leave Tobolsk for Moscow. As it turned out, the Tsar was prevented from getting any further than Ekaterinburg. The Tsarevich was too ill at that time to travel; the Tsar, it was decided, would leave first and the rest of the family would follow. Gibbes recalled his first encounter with Yakovlev:

> I was sitting by the Tsarevich's bed when the Emperor, accompanied by Yakovlev, looked at the Tsarevich. The Emperor said, 'This is my son and this is his tutor...' Yakovlev did not appear to be a man of culture. He looked more like a sailor.

Decorous English gentlemen found it particularly difficult to accept the social upheavals of the revolution. The British consul at Ekaterinburg, Thomas Preston, wrote of his dismay upon discovering that the Bolshevik governing body was to consist of no more than a gang of unruly young men in leather jackets.

A few days later Gibbes was again with the Tsarevich in his bedroom when the Empress informed him, in an undertone, that she had decided to accompany the Tsar. The Tsarevich overheard her, but remained silent. 'She was quite calm but her face showed traces of tears.' Unfailingly sensitive where the Imperial family were concerned, Gibbes left the room soon after. 'I thought that during the time they were preparing for the journey, they most probably would not care for the presence of a stranger.'

That evening everybody was invited to the Tsarina's boudoir, where tea was served. 'It was the most mournful and depressing party I ever attended,' recalled Gibbes. 'There was not much talking and no pretence at gaiety. It was solemn and tragic, a fit prelude to an inescapable tragedy.'

The maid, Anna Demidova, who would later be shot with the family, was quivering with fear. 'Oh Mr Gibbes!' she exclaimed 'I'm so frightened of the Bolsheviks, I don't know what they will do to us.' The Tsarina wrote in her diary 'Horrid to leave precious children.'

However, all was not, perhaps, as bleak as it appeared. Despite the withdrawal of the British government's invitation, the family still seemed to harbour hopes that they would eventually settle in England. Dr Botkin told his children he had been assured that, after a short trial in Moscow, the family would be free to go into exile. He was, they recalled, happier than he'd been since the beginning of the revolution; they cheerfully packed his tennis flannels in preparation for a future life in England. The party left between three and four o'clock in the morning. Gibbes managed to snatch a photograph of the carriages as they pulled away from the Governor's House.

Formal lessons were abandoned as the remaining members of the household concentrated on nursing Alexis back to health. Gibbes was particularly resourceful in his efforts to distract the invalid. He drew pictures on scraps of cardboard torn from two old boxes and found pieces of wire to make chains for a model ship.

His own last night at Tobolsk, a month later, was an altogether more jolly affair. He was to accompany the rest of the family to Ekaterinburg. There were two remaining bottles of good wine which could not be taken on the journey. It was decided to drink them at dinner, though this had been forbidden by the Commandant. There was great excitement when the Commandant was heard sneaking down the corridor:

We had only just time to hide the bottles and our glasses under the table hidden by a long trailing table cloth, when in he walked. He stood by the door and gave a quizzical look all round and we immediately all felt like little school boys caught doing something naughty at school... we could contain ourselves no longer but just burst out into a wild yell of uncontrollable laughter.

The three-day journey the next day from Tobolsk to Ekaterinburg began with an unsettled night on a steamer. Alexis was padlocked into his cabin with Nagorny, while the girls were not allowed to lock their doors. It was claimed later by a friend of one of the Bolshevik guards that the girls were molested during the night. There were even claims that the guards raped them.

When the steamer arrived at Tiumen, Gibbes was separated from the children and the party was divided in two. The children and courtiers were placed in a third-class carriage while the tutors and servants travelled in a cattle truck, unofficially classified as fourth class. Baroness Sophie Buxhoeveden wrote bitterly of the separation. Alexis, still in pain, was in need of distraction:

The Tsarevich lay all day, while we tried to amuse him as best we could... No entreaties however, would persuade Rodionoff [their Bolshevik guard] to allow either M. Gilliard or Mr Gibbes to join us in our carriage. Rodionoff seemed to enjoy refusing and vexing those in his power.

The train stopped briefly at Ekaterinburg station but then headed off into the outskirts of the town, where it was shunted backwards and forwards throughout the night. It finally came to a halt at about seven o'clock in the morning. Gibbes peered out of the window through a sheet of drizzle in order to see what was happening; he saw the children being ushered on to drozhkies for what would be their final journey to the House of Special Purpose.

The train then returned to the station where Gibbes and the other servants witnessed a riot as the Imperial boxes were unloaded. 'All these boxes contain the gold dresses of these wanton women!' screamed one woman. 'The Tsar has six pairs of boots and I have none,' cried a man, pointing to his bare feet: 'Death to the tyrant! Death to the bourgeois! Hang them, drown them in the lake.' On the side of Gibbes' carriage somebody scrawled: '17 servants of the Tyrant Nicholas'.

The 17 servants were, to their surprise, initially declared free. They were allowed to roam about the town during the day, though they were followed by soldiers wherever they went. Their nights were spent in the cramped train carriage. Most of the townspeople had no idea that the Imperial family were in Ekaterinburg. It took Gibbes, Gilliard and the Baroness Buxhoeveden several days to locate the House of Special Purpose. The house was, of course, under guard and they were not allowed to enter.

After about ten days, the servants were ordered to return to Tobolsk. They were to travel in the carriage they had been living in; their journey was to take three weeks and, as it turned out, they were to get no further than Tiumen. The first engine they hitched up to was delayed for ten days in a typhus-ridden village. They had to persuade the authorities to hook the carriage to a second engine. The unlikely group included the butler, various footmen, the Tsarina's second dresser Toutelberg and the aptly witty 'sauce artist' from the Imperial kitchen. The party was saved from hunger by a bag of potatoes thoughtfully supplied by the Tobolsk 'odd man'.

During the journey, Gibbes proved very popular as he turned out to be the only member of the party to travel with an enamel washing basin. While others contented themselves with the basin, Gibbes seized further opportunities for washing, with bathes in Siberian rivers.

'Mr Gibbes would rush into any stream that happened to be near a station...' recalled the Baroness. '...Those Siberian rivers are icy, so goodness knows into what temperature he had dipped when he came back, shivering but clean.'

Tiumen was in the hands of the Bolsheviks. All 17 former servants were obliged to carry papers which branded them as outlaws and forbade them from working. They found the people of Tiumen frightened to give them accommodation. Nevertheless, they did eventually find rooms: Gibbes, as in Tobolsk, on his own.

Decrees were posted every day on walls: those townsfolk who transgressed were 'to be relentlessly shot'. The Baroness reported that there was not much safety for women. There was even a period in Ekaterinburg when attempts were made to nationalise women; the idea was to redistribute the beautiful wives of rich merchants.

On 19 July the Whites liberated Tiumen. Ekaterinburg was liberated a week later. Gibbes and Gilliard went back to Ekaterinburg on the first available train and made their way to the House of Special Purpose. The shootings had taken place just days before – though how much either of the men had heard of what had happened is unclear.

**

The House of Special Purpose was situated near the centre of Ekaterinburg, on the side of a hill. It was built of white brick and heavy stone and had elaborate cornices. The Tsarina had described it as small; in fact it had 21 rooms. The first fence encircling the property reached the windows of the upper floor. Later, a second, outer fence was erected, reaching the eaves. The lower floor was made into guardrooms;

the upper floor formed a sort of prison. The square upon which the house stood, Ascension Square, was renamed The Square of National Vengeance.

Gibbes' feelings of dread and apprehension as he made his way, at last, through the gates and into the house cannot be doubted; nor his anguish upon finding the rooms in chilling disorder: hasty attempts had been made to burn the Imperial family's possessions; burnt remnants were strewn about the floors. The walls were covered with lewd slogans, cartoons of Rasputin and Alexandra were scrawled on the lavatory wall. His horror, finally, upon entering the blood-stained cellar must have been overwhelming.

However, the accounts he gave of his discoveries – both in his diary and at an official inquiry conducted by the White Russians – were remarkably dry. Perhaps this was owing to his hope, at the time, that the family had somehow survived. He clung to this hope for several months.

I found nothing out of the ordinary. The house was very much battered. The stoves were full of charred objects, such as portrait frames, all kinds of brushes and a little

76

basket in which the Tsarevich used to keep his hairbrush-es. A few things were scattered about, but I did not see many personal belongings.

He failed to mention one curious detail: as he walked through the echoing rooms, he picked up and pocketed a large assortment of keepsakes. He could have collected these scraps of paper and fragments of material in a fit of grief. Or he could have been pre-serving them simply for posterity. However, the most likely explanation is that he believed they possessed some kind of iconic value.

Certainly Gibbes treasured these mementoes – including some of Alexis' bloody bandages – for the rest of his life. He would have been gratified to know that, in 1993, the bandages were among items sent by the current owners of his collection – the Wernher Foundation – to Aldermaston, to help scientists con-ducting DNA tests on the Romanov bones.

Amongst the most poignant of Gibbes' discoveries was what is believed to be the last letter the Tsarevich ever wrote. It was to his friend, Dr Derevenko's son Kolya:

Dear Kolya,

All sisters send greetings to you, mother, and grandmother. I feel well myself. How is grandmother's health? What is [illegible] doing? My head was aching all day, but now the pain has gone completely. I embrace you warmly... Greetings to Botkins from all of us.

Always yours, Alexis.

Years later, in 1947, Gibbes received a sad letter from Kolya. Then living in Austria, he asked Gibbes to help him find a job in England. He asked Gibbes to pray 'for an unhappy man lost in a strange country'.

A few days later, Gilliard decided to return to Tiumen while Gibbes chose to settle in Ekaterinburg. No doubt Gibbes preferred his own company to that of Gilliard and the 15 other Imperial servants. But perhaps he also felt that, if he stayed in Ekaterinburg, he would be closer to the Imperial family.

Over the next few months, he returned again and again to the house. He steeled himself to spend hours in the cellar, conducting his own painstaking investi-

The Imperial family

gation. He found holes in the walls, created by bullets and bayonets. He took photographs of the holes and detailed notes of their positions on the walls. Again, he revealed little of himself in these notes. Later on, after the truth behind the shootings had been established, he would recall, with pain, the words of one of the witnesses: 'There was so much blood, they had to use a broom.'

A subsequent visit Gibbes received from the Tsar's valet, Terenty Chemodurov, exacerbated his fears for the family. Chemodurov had lived with the Romanovs in the House of Special Purpose before becoming ill and being sent to a prison hospital. He died a year later.

It seems that when the family had a special Easter cake, the Commissar cut himself big lumps wthout asking permission, and Chemodurov also mentioned rough treatment but it was very difficult for me to understand him as he wandered a little in his mind.

Just 18 months before, Gibbes had been a mainstay of the Russian Court, holding one of the most prestigious jobs in the whole of Russia. During and after the revolution, he would have found himself propelled along by the terrible urgency of each succeeding event. There now followed a strange hiatus. He was alone in Siberia, unemployed and without any clear direction. He found himself reduced to taking any teaching job that came his way. He reported to his Aunt Kate, with dry jauntiness, that he was making the best of 'teaching the unenlightened' of Ekaterinburg.

By October he had almost given up hope that the Imperial family were still alive. 'Although there is some chance that all may be well, I begin to fear the worst.' In November he was still regularly visiting the consul at Ekaterinburg, Thomas Preston, in the hope of gaining some concrete information.

It was through Preston that Gibbes finally received the offer of a proper job from the British High Commissioner, Sir Charles Eliot. From January 1919 Gibbes was to be a secretary on the staff at Omsk '£25 sterling monthly with board and lodging'. The lodging would at first consist of a compartment on Sir Charles' train. Faced with vast distances, not to mention the continually changing Red and White boundaries, military leaders found it more convenient to base themselves on trains. This particular train boasted a grand dining-car with a dining table and drawing-rooms.

In the meantime, life for Gibbes resumed some

kind of normality. Gilliard, frustrated in Tiumen, endlessly pestered Gibbes for news of the family: '*Tout le monde attend avec impatience pour avoir des nouvelles… N'avez vous pas reçu ma dernière lettre?*' he demanded. Gibbes eventually wrote to Gilliard, but most of this letter concerned not the family but the Baroness. He had lent her 1,300 roubles but she was insisting she had no memory of the transaction. Gilliard had witnessed the early negotiations and Gibbes sought his help. The Baroness' fall from grace in Gibbes' view was complete. '*Je savais qu' elle était avare,*' he ranted in his letter, '*mais je n'ai jamais pensé qu'elle pourrait aller si loin.*'

While occasionally given to melancholy and health worries, Gibbes does not seem to have suffered from morbid fears. Was he underestimating the seriousness of his situation or was he simply demonstrating, once again, his slightly bull-headed bravery? He appeared surprised when he heard that the British Foreign Office had sent a telegram to Thomas Preston – at the close of 1918 – asking if Gibbes were dead or alive. 'It makes one realise what a narrow escape we all had,' he commented. On 21 January

1919, the Foreign Office was finally able to reassure Gibbes' Uncle Will that they had received word from the Acting British Consul in Ekaterinburg: 'Mr Gibbes is still in that town and is in good health.'

Throughout his correspondence of early 1919 there is an infelicitous juxtaposition of gravity and frivolity. In January he wrote to another of the Imperial family's teachers, Klavdia Bitner, in Tobolsk. He wrote delicately of the Imperial family: 'I am told there is little real doubt as to the fate of those we love but at the same time it is not yet proved.'

However, later in the same letter he addressed other preoccupations. 'Do you remember the beautiful crucifix you got Denesov to carve for me? Might I ask you to get him to do another? I should also like the kind of comb he made for Anna Stepanovna [Demidova, the maid who died with the family]. He makes very nice combs and the other man's were very bad.'

His decision to send his Uncle Will pictures of the Imperial family in the hope of selling them to a newspaper was perhaps slightly precipitate. His accompanying letter demonstrated his great concern about the copywriting of the material. 'They might be published in one of the best papers which do that kind of work... I thought I might be able to give some lecture or even make a small book.' These proposals sit uneasily with the objections Gibbes later raised against Gilliard's writing of his memoirs. He does, however, acknowledge the moral question with a sort of apology: 'I have lost so much by the Russian catastrophe that I feel obliged to realise my few available assets although it almost seems like the sale of old heirlooms to do so.'

Though Gibbes appeared, by the spring of 1919, to have accepted that the Imperial family had all perished, he may still have harboured the barest of hopes that some or all of them had survived. These would have suffered a final blow when the leader of the official White inquiry, Nicholas Sokolov, unearthed evidence pointing to a burial site. He summoned Gibbes to help identify objects – including human remains – brought up from a mine-shaft at the Four Brothers. 'All who actually took part in the investigation and inspected the remains, were obliged to abandon hope that anyone had survived,' Gibbes later commented.

The bodies of the family and retainers were initially thrown down the mine. Near the site, buried in leaves and mud, lay various items, including Dr Botkin's false teeth. The first investigators had been puzzled to find piles of eggshells lying around the site. It turned out that, the day before the shooting, the Bolshevik guard had asked nuns supplying food for the Imperial family to bring 50 eggs. The eggs were handed to the Romanovs' chef, Khariotonov, who dutifully boiled them. The 50 boiled eggs were to be eaten the next day by the chef's own killers, feasting next to two funeral pyres.

In fact, it was discovered years later that nine of the 11 bodies were subsequently levered out of the Four Brothers mine and buried in a shallow grave. Two bodies – believed to be those of the Tsarevich and Anastasia – remain missing.

Gibbes was nearly overcome with sorrow as he examined the debris laid out roughly on a tarpaulin. The description he gave afterwards was the more powerful for its understatement. 'Naturally, I gave them all the help I could, but it was painful to see some of the insignificant trifles which had no meaning for anybody else but which meant so much to me.' Among the trifles was an assortment of nails, tinfoil and copper coins which nobody was able to place, until Gibbes reminded Sokolov of Alexis' passion for collecting odds and ends.

On 21 July 1919, he described to his Aunt Kate how he had identified Jimmy, the King Charles spaniel given to Anastasia by Anna Vryubova. Alexis's dog, Joy (another male), survived the shooting but was believed to have been blinded by the trauma of what he had witnessed. Among the human remains was a portion of a finger severed at the second joint. Gibbes' report is, as usual, restrained, with no intimation of the disgust and horror he must have felt:

> As I saw it lying in spirit it looked to me like Dr Botkin's finger but it was probably swollen, for medical experts have declared it to be the third finger of a lady no longer quite young, and it is held to be that of the late Empress.

Later, in a letter contesting the claims of one of the false grand duchesses, he wrote that he had seen six corsets. 'Four pairs of larger size had evidently belonged to the Empress, the two elder grand duchesses and the faithful Demidova. The two smaller ones could only have belonged to the Grand Duchesses Marie and Anastasia.' A photograph exists of Gibbes at the mine. The *Times* correspondent, Robert Wilton, is peering down the shaft while Gibbes stands slightly apart, a stiff figure in a neatly belted coat.

During the court proceedings of the inquiry in July 1919, Wilton particularly noted that Gibbes betrayed no emotion as he spoke. Gibbes would probably have been proud of the triumph of propriety over pain. He commented on the eye-witness accounts of the shootings:

At such a solemn and tragic moment the Empress and the Grand Duchess Tatiana Nikolaevna would certainly have fallen on their knees in prayer and their example would have been followed by all the other members of the Family and Household. Yakimov's evidence that Demidova [the maid] 'kept on running about and hid herself behind a pillow' conveys a peculiarly vivid scene of which it is difficult not to believe he was an eye-witness. Demidova was a tall, well-built woman... who, in direct contrast to her physical appearance, was of a singularly timid and shrinking disposition which recoiled from the sight of suffering.

To Aunt Kate he wrote laconically of a service held in Ekaterinburg to commemorate the anniversary of the shooting: 'On the 17th of this month we had a memorial service in the Cathedral here. It was extremely sad.'

In July 1919 Ekaterinburg was recaptured by the Reds and Sokolov was obliged to abandon his investigation for the last time. He packed the remains from the Four Brothers mine-shaft in one of the Tsarina's boxes. The box was stored for a while at the British Consulate at Harbin. Gibbes himself was believed to have been in charge of it at one point. In 1920 Sokolov wrote to Gibbes – 'My dear Sydney Ivanovich' – requesting British safeguards for the box. But in the end the British government refused to take it; it was taken in by the chief of the French Military Mission.

Throughout 1919, Gibbes longed to return to England. In February he wrote wistfully to Winifred from the British High Commission in Vladivostok. 'I don't know when I shall get home... Most of the staff is leaving more or less shortly – weary, goodness knows I am, but I can't talk about that.' In a subsequent letter, he wrote of the possibility of going round the world to get home. 'In ordinary circumstances that would have been very nice but one hardly feels disposed to enjoy oneself in any way nowadays.'

For 18 months he heard no news from England. When finally he received a letter from Winifred, in May, he was afraid to open it. 'Thank heaven you are all well,' he began in reply. It was clear from the same letter that at 43 he had not yet acquired a taste for conventional fun: 'The High Commission is giving a ball tomorrow evening. I detest such things so that the event will not give me any particular pleasure.'

When the British High Commission in Siberia came to an end, Gibbes left for Peking, where he served as a secretary at the British Embassy. At this stage he obviously envisaged a career in the diplomatic service; in November 1919 he had written to Sir Charles Eliot requesting recommendations for consulate posts. However, after only a brief stint in Peking, Gibbes' future was again uncertain.

Sir Charles Eliot now suggested a job with the Chinese Maritime Customs in Harbin. It could not have been the prestigious job Gibbes was hoping for; as one of his relations pointed out, he was merely 'an assistant to an assistant'. But Gibbes took an immediate liking to Harbin; he was to spend nearly 20 years of his life there. He gave his first keenly observed impressions to his Aunt Kate: 'The Chinese seem to swarm everywhere like ants more than human beings, but they are so merry and bright, so smiling and cheerful, so knowing and inquisitive, crowding round you if ever you stop so that you feel they are crawling all over you.' He found the Chinese were frightened of his camera, running away shrieking with laughter whenever he produced it.

It was in a Russian shop in Harbin, in 1922, that Gibbes first set eyes on the 16-year-old Russian boy who was to become his adopted son, George Paveliev. The boy was working in a shop selling goods belonging to newly impoverished White Russians. George approached Gibbes asking if he could find him work in the Customs Office. Through the American consul, Gibbes managed to find George work with an American buyer of raw furs.

George was Moscow-born, the son of a White Russian civil engineer. As a young boy, his parents had taken him to Shanghai before installing him in a boarding school there. After the revolution he had lost touch with them. He had tried, at one point, to return to Russia but fled back over the border after witnessing terrible atrocities. He swore he had seen Cossacks throw live bodies into engines for fuel.

Gibbes and the boy became very close. Having made a point of living alone most of his adult life, Gibbes now invited George to join him on his houseboat. He grew to love George, but whether there was anything sexual in the nature of his love cannot be known. Certainly George, though profoundly grateful to his adoptive father, never displayed any tendency towards homosexuality. He married twice and was, according to his own two sons, an enthusiastic ladies' man.

It is possible that Gibbes never examined the nature of his attachment to George. His own sexuality may have remained a puzzle to him. In his dream diary he recorded, with no comment, an intriguing dream involving a young boy called Nikolai (written in Cyrillic letters), Miss Cade and a large spider:

> I was in bed, very far off was Miss C and next to me was Nikolai... suddenly I heard the noise of something crawling upstairs and a big spider... crawled up the wall behind my bed and down the bed between me and Nikolai.

Two years after they met, Gibbes formally adopted George. Why he should have particularly chosen George out of all the abandoned children in Manchuria will always remain a mystery. George's elder son, Charles Gibbes Paveliev, thinks perhaps it was to do with his father's appealing zest for life.

George's real parents eventually escaped from Russia and arrived in Harbin in 1934, but by this time George, now 28, had settled in England. Sadly they both died within three months of their arrival and were never reunited with their son.

***

Unfortunately Gibbes' work as a customs officer was to prove unrewarding. He felt increasingly that he was existing in a moral and spiritual vacuum. He was obliged to make frequent visits to a battle-zone in Manchouli; on one of these forays, he lost his way in a blizzard and was reduced to eating frozen mangoes which he thawed by sitting on them.

Throughout his correspondence with Gilliard, in the late 1920s, he talked of his pressing need for rest. He described the onset of his recurring sickness poetically: '*En route de Chine je me suis tombé malade, pas subitement mais peu a peu comme un vieux meuble qui s'ecrase.*'

Putting aside any quibbles of the past, Gilliard and his wife – the Romanovs' former nanny Alexandra Tegleva, whom he married in 1922 – were insistent that Gibbes should visit them in Lausanne. He agreed to come, providing, he insisted, that no one was told of his visit. Perhaps this was a veiled allusion to Gilliard's venture into public life with his memoirs. The visit seems to have been a success. Afterwards Gilliard wrote that he did not feel Gibbes had changed much in appearance, except for his white hair. This, he added, was a great triumph, in view of all the suffering he had been through.

But at around this time Gibbes fell gravely ill and nearly died. He had been travelling from Harbin to England for a holiday when he was struck down in the Philippines with gallstones and a subsequent infection. He wired George, who was by then in Australia on a sheep ranch (he did not move to England until 1931). George came immediately; Gibbes always believed that George saved his life.

The illness and three-month convalescence were to form a turning-point in Gibbes' life. The enforced inactivity drove him into self-reflection; this, in turn, led him to several resolutions concerning his spiritual life. He would bring his inner life to order and he would then try to reconcile his inner life with his outer life by embracing some form of established religion. His initial idea was to become an Anglican priest. When he finally reached England, he wrote to Anna Vyrubova, telling her that he was no longer enjoying living in China. He said he wanted to return to England for good:

> I spent some terms at St Stephen's House which is an institution for preparing candidates for ordination in the Church of England. Nevertheless it is not so easy at my time of life to undergo the training necessary and I am now without influence or protection of any kind that might ease the toilsome path in that direction.

However, in 1934 he finally decided he would become a member of the Russian Orthodox Church; his conversion, in Harbin, would be swiftly followed by his ordination. Why he had rejected, once again, the Anglican church is unclear. But he had been profoundly impressed by the unfailing faith of the Imperial family; perhaps it was inevitable that he should finally adopt their particular religion.

He passed through his early degrees under the name of Alexei, in honour of the Tsarevich. In a letter to Winifred, he expressed his feelings about embracing Orthodoxy. It was, he said, 'like getting home after a long journey'. Years later Gibbes' niece reveals that his siblings – two of his sisters had married Anglican clergymen – were 'quite shattered' by his decision.

In December 1934 Gibbes took his vows. He became a monk on the 15th, was ordained deacon on the 19th and priest on the 23rd. From now on he would be known as Father Nicholas (he took the name in honour of the Tsar). Many of those attending the ordination were beleaguered White Russians who had lost everything in the revolution – some of them openly wept. 'All the church was in tears... I was overcome,' he confessed afterwards to Winifred.

He wrote to his newly acquired godmother, Elizabeth Nicolaevna, of his sadness at losing the name Alexei: 'I loved and love dear Saint Alexei and it was a bond with him who we have lost and who was dearer to me than them all.' As an elderly man, he would tell his friend, David Beattie, that he had always felt sad when he was away from the Tsarevich.

He moved from the Oriental Hotel, where he was now based, to Dom Miloserdia, 'House of Mercy'.

His days were spent attending church services, giving lessons in one of the secondary schools, attending theological courses and taking private lessons in Slavonic four times a week. His correspondence hereafter inevitably contained increasing references to religion. At one point it seemed imperative that he should return to England, as George was threatened with deportation. Father Nicholas had by then installed him in a fruit farm in Stourmouth, in Kent. '...if my desire is pleasing to God He will protect George in the present distressing circumstances, and if it is not pleasing to God it is better it come to an end immediately.'

In March 1935, Father Nicholas became an abbot. The Holy Synod remarked that he was the first English Orthodox Abbot in history. He immediately passed on the news to Elizabeth Nicolaevna; so excited was he that he momentarily forgot his commitment to humility. He kept a rough draft of his letter:

You will ['perhaps' added above in pencil] have seen in the newspapers that ['unworthy as I am' added above in pencil] the Metropolitan Anthony has raised me to the

dignity of an abbot... I chased all over Harbin to get a
suitable pectoral cross and with great difficulty found one
that I liked.

***

Father Nicholas had for some time now believed
that his duty lay in founding some kind of Anglo-
Orthodox organisation in England. As he wrote to a
Count Grabbe: 'It has long been my earnest hope that
the Anglican Church should put herself right with the
Holy Orthodox church.' He set his heart upon an
unlikely scheme involving the conversion of George's
fruit farm into a monastic foundation.

He finally returned to England in 1937. The Gibbs
family doubtless welcomed him back, though his
adoption of George remained a difficulty for them.
'They thought it strange,' comments his niece. By
this time, George was successfully growing goose-
berries, apples and pears as well as breeding poultry.
He had placed an advertisement for a chicken hus-
bandry expert in the local paper, and the lady who
applied for the job, Doris, was to become his wife; the

couple married in 1939. Father Nicholas had agreed to perform the ceremony but, on the day of the wedding, changed his mind. George's son, Charles, suggests that he may not have realised, until the last moment, that the bride was a divorcee. The couple were to have two sons, Charles and Andrew.

Charles' strongest recollections of Father Nicholas – or 'F. N.' as he was known to the boys – involve awkward Sunday lunches: 'The radio was switched off and we were told to mind our manners.' The memory is shared by his younger brother, Andrew: 'The atmosphere was electric.' Andrew remembers, at the age of eight, being asked by Father Nicholas what he was reading. 'When I said "Enid Blyton", he said, "You should be reading Walter Scott."'

However, Charles remembers being read 'Biggles' by his adoptive grandfather at Christmas. Andrew, in turn, recalls that Father Nicholas used to save his sweet rations for the boys. They would receive six months' worth of sweets on their birthdays. Both men recall the mixture of pride and embarrassment they felt as they accompanied their adoptive grandfather through the streets in his Orthodox robes.

He now had long flowing white hair and beard. Though he never quite mastered his temper, he had acquired something of a mellow charm. In later photographs his eyes seem to shine with a gentle warmth, the flawless skin softened with wrinkles. He smiles broadly, his sizeable teeth bared but happily foreshortened by lavish moustaches. George Katkov's daughter, Tanya Joyce, remembers children in Oxford calling him – not altogether affectionately – 'Father Christmas'. Today, Andrew laughs before summoning his own image: 'He looked like the grandfather of Dracula.'

Unfortunately, George's wife soon began to feel that Father Nicholas was interfering too much in their family life. There had been a particularly awkward time when he tried to go ahead with his plan to convert the farm into a monastic foundation. There were no objections as he changed the oast-house into a sort of hermit's cell, where he slept and prayed. But he then set about converting the family drawing-room into a chapel in which he insisted on holding daily services.

After several tense months, Father Nicholas aban-

Father Nicholas

doned the foundation project, but his keen interest in developments at the farm never abated. When the couple were divorced in 1969 – six years after Father Nicholas' death – he was mentioned in the proceedings. Mrs Justice Lane granted a decree nisi: 'It is impossible to avoid the conclusion that Father Nicholas must have known of the unhappiness he was causing in this marriage...' Andrew's recollection is muted. 'I think my mother did feel that at times my father paid more attention to Father Nicholas than he did to her. It seemed that if Father Nicholas had a problem, Dad was round there in five seconds.'

When the Second World War was declared, Father Nicholas was attached to the parish of St Philip on Buckingham Palace Road. But during the Blitz he moved out to Oxford, where he established a church at Bartlemas Chapel, off the Cowley Road. He succeeded in acquiring a loyal following and this should have been a fruitful and happy time for him. But his wartime diary entries are unilluminating: '*November 15 1943*: Cabbages for pickling... *August 20 1944*: Spent day at home. Weather indifferent.' However these are less dour than entries, postwar, in 1949: '*February 11*: Lav blocked again... *August 4*: Unwell... *August 5*: Unwell but up.'

It was during one of the services at Bartlemas that Father Nicholas first spotted Clive Feary, a handsome boy of 15 who was to become one of his last great friends: 'Father Nicholas came up to me after the service, wanting to know who I was. I was flattered by his interest.' The boy was a keen Russophile and he and Father Nicholas quickly discovered shared interests. They began to meet regularly over Father Nicholas' vegetable soups and cabbage pies. Within a year Clive had converted to Orthodoxy, changing his name to Dmitri. At one stage he even took rooms in Father Nicholas' house in Marston Street.

For a while, the unlikely couple seemed inseparable. They travelled together between London, where Father Nicholas had a house, and Oxford. Dmitri – who has now adopted his wife's name, Kornhardt – remembers him taking a large black bag everywhere with him; in the bag he carried house-shoes and a collection of newspapers gathered up at railway and bus stations.

Father Nicholas evidently had not lost his taste for cleanliness. Dmitri recalls, with pleasure, that he frequently washed his face and that his hands shone. He was a regular visitor to the Turkish Baths in Great Russell Street. In his London house he created a rudimentary and dangerous sauna comprising an electric heater rigged up in a cubicle.

There was, however, an occasional sternness in Father Nicholas' manner to Dmitri. At one point, Dmitri was obliged to carry out his National Service in the Merchant Navy. His church attendance became irregular, and, when he finally turned up at Bartlemas, he received an unexpectedly severe reprimand: 'You're wandering about. When you're here you don't care to come to church. You're MEAN with your time.'

Following the revolution, the Russian Orthodox Church had suffered years of persecution at the hands of the Soviets. Now, in the early 1940s, Stalin issued his policy of religious toleration. The issue of the policy resulted in a split within the Church. One faction, the Mother Church, was willing to establish and maintain links with the Soviet Union; the other, the Church in Exile, remained resolutely anti-Soviet. In 1945, Father Nicholas declared his allegiance to the Mother Church. In common with other Church leaders, he felt it was right that the Russian Orthodox Church should operate under the auspices of Moscow.

Father Nicholas' decision created discord among his followers: the monarchists looked upon it as a betrayal. There were rumours among some of the notoriously sensitive Orthodox leaders that, in return for pledging his allegiance to the Soviets, he had been awarded some kind of pension. According to Dmitri and Charles, he did indeed receive packages from the Soviet Union. But these contained nothing more than calendars, biscuits and caviar in blue tins.

Three years later, Father Nicholas was obliged to move from Bartlemas. He bought three terraced cottages and a large adjoining building in Marston Street. In the adjoining building he created a chapel which became a sort of shrine to the Romanovs. From the ceiling hung the chandelier that had been in the grand duchesses' bedroom at Ekaterinburg. Along the walls Father Nicholas lined up the icons he had salvaged from fireplaces and dustbins after the assassinations. In the altar area he installed a pair of the Tsar's felt boots.

***

By the end of the 1940s, Father Nicholas' growing following included the eminent historian George Katkov. Katkov's daughter, Dr Tanya Joyce, keeps a picture of Father Nicholas, or 'Fuffy', as the Katkovs called him, on the wall of the living-room of her house in Headington. 'After the war, my father brought DPs – displaced persons – from Russian camps. These people were traumatised; some of them were terrifying. Father Nicholas was one of the very few adults I knew who wasn't frightening,' recalls Tanya.

But if he was not frightening, Father Nicholas never quite mastered the priestly art of disseminating calm. Both Tanya and Charles recall the awkwardness of having to make their first confessions. 'He didn't know how to put an 11-year-old at ease,' says Tanya ruefully. 'Poor bloke, it was extremely embarrassing for both of us.'

According to Charles, one of the few women whom Father Nicholas respected was Professor Elisabeth Koutaissoff, an Oxford don. Her name crops up in his diaries in the early 1940s.

Now in her nineties and in a nursing home,

Professor Koutaissoff has lost little of the acuity Father Nicholas so much admired. Her sentiments are expressed precisely, in dispassionate tones. She was impressed by Father Nicholas' loyalty to the Romanovs and by his courageous decision to follow them into exile. However, she did not think he had a proper religious calling. 'He was following his faithfulness to the Imperial family. You have to come to the priesthood through God, not emotion.'

But she also thought him inefficient. His organisation of the services at Marston Street was, by all accounts, erratic. He would leave somewhat cavalier notices pinned to the door: 'Gone away to Kent. No liturgy this Sunday'.

One Russian priest, Father Michael Fortonnatto, recalls attending a service at which Father Nicholas was unable to offer Communion. 'When Father Nicholas came out with the exclamation "Draw near", it became clear that there was nothing left in the chalice. He had not expected us and he had to apologise. I was... well... a little taken aback.' At one point Father Nicholas became convinced that his icons had miraculously begun to shine. 'Not since the days of the persecution has such a thing come to pass,' he proclaimed. But an elderly woman parishioner put the miracle down to no more than her own assiduously applied detergent.

Bishop Kallistos of Diokleia, an eminent Orthodox leader based in Oxford, smiles fondly as he recalls Father Nicholas: 'He was the cat who walked by himself.'

Bishop Kallistos' view is that Father Nicholas was respected within Oxford's Russian community, but not always taken seriously: 'People didn't quite know where to place him.' He once saw a picture of Father Nicholas on the front of the *Church Times*. A service had been held to raise funds for Russian refugees coming to England after the Second World War. 'There was Father Nicholas looking soulful and sad. The text read: "This refugee, far from his native land, thinks sadly of happier days gone by..." This was a Yorkshireman,' adds Bishop Kallistos, eyes shining with mirth. He admits that Father Nicholas would probably also have been amused.

In 1952, Father Nicholas acquired an assistant at Marston Street. Basil Krivoschein was the son of

Stolypin's Minister of Agriculture. Stolypin was the great pre-revolutionary reformer assassinated in 1911. Basil Krivoschein had spent 25 years on Mount Athos and had then been arrested by the Greek government. While in captivity, he had his two blessing fingers cut off. Father Nicholas was instrumental in his eventual escape to England.

Within two years of his arrival, Father Nicholas had arranged for Basil's ordination and appointed him chaplain. Father Basil was a great success. An old *nyanya* of Professor Koutaissoff was particularly moved after being given Communion by him: 'That was a real priest,' she exclaimed.

In the late 1950s, Father Nicholas collapsed during a service. One of his parishioners recalls him struggling to finish the service: 'He appealed to us: "I can't go on – you must take over."' Some parishioners immediately formed a committee and offered to buy Marston Street. Father Nicholas rejected their offer. 'I could get more on the open market,' he complained to Dmitri. The newly formed committee then decided to set up an alternative place of worship in Canterbury Road. 'We never meant to take away all that Father Nicholas was trying to do,' insisted one former committee member. 'Our original plan was only to have services on days when there was no service at Marston Street.'

However, Father Nicholas was unable to view the Canterbury Road project – now The Orthodox Church of the Holy Trinity and the Annunciation – as anything but hostile. His staunchest adherents followed his lead; the rift between the two factions continued after his death, with some former parishioners choosing to attend services in London rather than venture into the Canterbury Road church.

At one stage, early on in the proceedings, Father Basil made the mistake of attending a meeting in connection with the new venture. Father Nicholas was furious. 'He was hurt and disappointed,' Dmitri recalls. 'He felt betrayed.' Afterwards, Father Nicholas turned Father Basil out of Marston Street, leaving him with his luggage on the doorstep.

Dmitri himself recalls several serious rows with Father Nicholas, mostly concerning the Romanovs. 'I once said the Romanovs were killed for political reasons. He said: "You are trying to justify killing. Thou shalt not kill. You don't seem to change and some-times you seem to favour the Bolsheviks."' The pair argued fiercely about capital punishment. 'I said "an eye for an eye". He turned on me sharply: "That's Old Testament. People haven't changed since they cried Barabbas."'

Capital punishment was repugnant to Father Nicholas. In 1953, he took Dmitri to pray outside Wandsworth Prison when Derek Bentley was exe-cuted. Bentley, a 19-year-old epileptic with the mental age of 11, was executed for his tangential role in the killing of a policeman. At the time of the execution there were riots, with protestors demonstrating for and against the death penalty. Dmitri admits that he felt intimidated.

'Father Nicholas said silent prayers for Derek Bentley's soul; he would have thought it ostentatious to pray aloud. We arrived at the prison gates ten minutes before the execution and stayed 15 minutes afterwards... It felt like hours.' When Ruth Ellis was hanged, Father Nicholas went to pray outside the gates again. That time he went alone.

***

The following year, in 1954, Father Nicholas took the momentous step of agreeing to meet Anna Anderson, the woman who claimed to be the Grand Duchess Anastasia. It is not known what persuaded him, at the age of 78, to meet her. Gilliard had been trying to bring about a meeting for nearly 30 years. Father Nicholas may have felt it was his duty to meet her before he died. Perhaps he harboured a niggling hope that she really was Anastasia. In any case, he agreed to travel to Paris and spend several days in her company.

Arguments surrounding various claimants had raged ever since 1918. Indeed, Father Nicholas recalled one story circulating even before the shootings. He remembered a report in the *Daily Graphic* in 1917, asserting that the Grand Duchess Tatiana had escaped to America. He said he watched Tatiana as she read the revelations; the pair were sitting together in the drawing-room at Tobolsk.

Over the years, all five of the Imperial children

miraculously reappeared. Once the Tsar himself was spotted walking around London, his hair snow-white. On one particularly bizarre occasion in America, a false Anastasia found herself reunited with a false Alexis. The potential for mutual embarrassment was obvious but the would-be siblings apparently carried off a reunion with the requisite emotion. They saw each other three times over the next few weeks but, perhaps unsurprisingly, never met again.

Anna Anderson, then known as Madame Tchaikovsky, had been pulled from a canal in Berlin in 1920. For the rest of her life she claimed she was the Grand Duchess Anastasia and that she had been rescued by one of the shooting squad in Ekaterinburg.

Her most fervent supporter was Gleb Botkin, son of Dr Botkin, who insisted that she recognised pictures he had drawn for Anastasia in Siberia. He fought her cause all his life and in his memoirs included an unappealing photograph of her with the caption: 'The Grand Duchess as she is today'.

Upon first seeing Anna Anderson, the Swiss tutor

Gilliard and his wife were also both persuaded that she was Anastasia. Gilliard's wife, a former nanny to the Imperial children, examined Anderson's feet and swore she had the same foot malformation as Anastasia; Gilliard himself was sufficiently convinced to talk to a surgeon about the condition of 'Her Imperial Highness'.

Subsequently the scales fell from both their eyes. Gilliard later even wrote a book *The False Anastasia*. In a complete *volte face*, he insisted that he had known immediately that she was a fraud. In his letters to Father Nicholas through the 1920s, Gilliard harped on endlessly about the *'lutte contre l'aventurière Tchaikowski'*. As early as January 1929, Gilliard wrote saying he had received documents from the German police stating that she was a Polishwoman called Schanzkowski. Sixty five years later, in 1994, DNA tests finally proved that she was, indeed, Franziska Schanzkowska.

In 1928, Father Nicholas wrote his own measured objection: 'In my opinion there is unfortunately no room for doubt that the Grand Duchess Anastasia perished at Ekaterinburg.' On a lighter note, he rather enjoyed contesting Anna Anderson's claim that he had a limp. 'Happily in full possession of both my legs I am able to demonstrate that I limp only in the imagination of Mme Tchaikovsky.'

In her book *I Anastasia*, published by Penguin seven years after their meeting, Anna Anderson wisely left out the limp. Instead, she mentioned twice that 'Mr Gibbes' was inclined to tilt his head to one side. She had obviously seen photographs in which he was inclined, indeed, to tilt his head rather awkwardly.

Father Nicholas reached the house designated for his fateful meeting late one afternoon in November. What were his thoughts as he contemplated meeting Anna Anderson? Did he wonder if he were really about to be reunited with Anastasia? Was he haunted by his last sight of the 17-year-old Anastasia, heaving her bags through the rain outside Ekaterinburg?

The first signs were not promising. Upon arrival, Father Nicholas was told that everybody in the house would have to wear masks because 'Anastasia' was ill. In the end the stricture could not be adhered to: there were no masks to hand.

After the meeting, he wrote a detailed but charac-
teristically sober affidavit:

> After dinner I was taken for my first interview to the room
> the so-called Grand Duchess Anastasia and her German
> companion were occupying. The room contained two sin-
> gle beds in which the two women lay. They spent the
> whole of the five days in the house and every time I saw
> them they were still in bed and I never saw them dressed
> at any time.
>
> The so-called Grand Duchess Anastasia looked at me
> suspiciously over the top of a newspaper which she con-
> tinued to hold on all occasions in front of her face so that
> only her eyes and hair were visible. This tactic she contin-
> ued to use every time I saw her and never permitted me of
> her own will to see the whole of her face.
>
> From behind the newspaper she stretched forth her
> hand and gave me the tips of her fingers to shake. Such
> features as were visible did not correspond in any way
> with those of the Grand Duchess I had known, and I con-
> sider that, even bearing in mind the years that had passed
> between 1918 and 1954, the Grand Duchess Anastasia
> whom I knew could not have become anything like the
> woman now calling herself the Grand Duchess Anastasia.

I showed her six photographs which I had taken with me. She looked at each and shook her head and indicated that they meant nothing to her. These pictures actually were of some of the rooms in which the Grand Duchess Anastasia had lived, of the pet dog with which she had played, and of the teachers who had taught her...

On the last time I saw the so-called Grand Duchess to say goodbye to her, I was able to approach nearer to her and look over the top of the paper, and saw her whole face and in particular her right ear. Her right ear does not in any way resemble the right ear of the true Grand Duchess Anastasia as I have a photograph of her which clearly displays the ear and its peculiar shape... I am quite satisfied that she is an impostor.

Afterwards he revealed that he had also asked her what costume she was wearing when she burst into his classroom at Tsarskoe Selo, the morning after the fancy-dress ball. Her answer – 'I was a columbine, wasn't I naughty?' – was, of course, wrong. Tanya Joyce remembers Father Nicholas telling her father about it. 'He came back in a great state of excitement. He said, "The lady was a charlatan and I was able to expose it." ' Father Nicholas' most often quoted pronouncement on Anna Anderson was simply: 'If that woman is Anastasia, I'm a Chinaman.'

***

From 1955 to 1957, Nicholas Garland, later to become the *Daily Telegraph* political cartoonist, rented rooms from Father Nicholas in Robert Street. He was then an art student. Garland was captivated and intrigued by Father Nicholas; he liked him. While Father Nicholas never entirely lost his propensity for fallings-out, he seems, latterly, to have developed an un-Soames-like aptitude for companionship. Garland recalls being as much struck by Father Nicholas' Merlin-like appearance as his mode of selecting lodgers. 'He asked to see our hands. He then held them, peering narrowly at the palms. Then he looked up: "All right, you can come in."'

Father Nicholas inhabited a cell-like basement room containing a bed, stove and innumerable icons. 'His room was no bigger than a box,' recalls another former student. 'If you sat with him you were virtually knee to knee.' His lodgers, mainly young male art students from the Slade, found him a benevolent landlord. He was fatherly in his attitude towards them, cheerfully overlooking noise and outlandish wall decorations. He reacted mildly even when one student gouged holes in a treasured table with a nail.

They found George, who occasionally checked on his adoptive father's property, much more intimidating. Father Nicholas' only rule for the students was not to damage the carpets; he had brought them all the way back from Russia, he told them.

In his later years, Father Nicholas became increasingly eccentric. One cause of malaise would have been his mixed feelings over his professed allegiance to the Mother Church. In 1958, Bishop Kallistos saw him celebrating his name-day with nuns attached to the Church in Exile. 'The nuns were severe in their view of the Mother Church and what they saw as the Mother Church's collaboration with the Communists. But there he was, sitting at the head of the table. He was even asked to bless the table.'

On a more mundane level, his previously high standards of cleanliness and tidiness began to slip. In the kitchen at Marston Street, vegetable soup was continually on the boil. When it began to get low, more vegetables were simply added on top. A Greek Archbishop who came from London to visit Father Nicholas was so horrified by the state of the kitchen that he refused to accept even a cup of tea. 'Father Nicholas was very hurt,' says one parishioner. 'I felt sorry for him.'

As for the chapel, it was overwhelmed with clutter, broken chairs and old newspapers. There was even a couple of redundant pianos, bought by Father Nicholas as bargains. On one occasion, four parishioners decided to clean the chapel while Father Nicholas was away. Among the more unusual items they came upon was a figurine of a nude woman under one of the side tables. When Father Nicholas returned and found black rubbish bags piled up in front of the chapel he was enraged; for several weeks he conducted no services and the congregation was obliged to meet in the drawing-room of one of the parishioners.

David Beattie was among the last people Father Nicholas met in whom he confided. At the time of their meeting, in 1961, Beattie was a student of

Russian at Lincoln College, Oxford; he was greatly impressed by the elderly priest. He subsequently collected and maintained a file of papers concerning Father Nicholas, and kept detailed notes of their three lengthy meetings.

He first encountered Father Nicholas in a vicarage garden in Bethnal Green; Beattie had just returned from Moscow, where he had been acting as an interpreter at the first British Trade and Industry Fair. Father Nicholas would then have been aged 85. 'He was dressed in what can only be described as rags, carrying an enormous disreputable-looking bag. He looked like a benevolent fairytale gnome.' Beattie remembers Father Nicholas as worldly, preoccupied with his various rented properties. Indeed, on the second occasion that they met, Father Nicholas was trying to sell two of his cottages, as he was forbidden by law to raise the rents. 'He was utterly practical. He was no mystic.'

Father Nicholas amused Beattie by swearing that his Heath Robinson-esque sauna kept him young:

Father Nicholas said, 'Have you observed the ways of the

serpent? Every now and again the serpent sheds its skin. That's exactly what I do... I wait till the cubicle is very hot. I take off all my clothes and pour water over myself and sit in the cubicle. Very soon all my skin falls off and I come out young again.'

More unusually, Father Nicholas was willing to talk to Beattie about the Romanovs. All Father Nicholas' close friends would have been aware of the power the family continued to wield over him. He once wrote in a letter that his most cherished possession was his memory of the Imperial family on their road to Calvary: 'so sweet', he wrote, 'so sad'. At every service conducted in Marston Street, the Tsar, Tsarina, Tsarevich and Grand Duchesses were commemorated. Father Nicholas conducted services in memory of the family during which the tears would course down his face. Dmitri was struck by the rapidity with which Father Nicholas would recover himself after these betrayals of emotion: 'In the next second, he would be smiling,' he muses affectionately. According to Dmitri, Father Nicholas once fell to the floor in an emotional collapse; this created a problem, as none of the female worshippers was allowed into the altar area. Dmitri and Father Nicholas' friend, Serge Bolshakoff, were obliged to help him to his feet as best they could.

Behind the chapel Father Nicholas had a library-study in which he displayed photographs he had taken in Tsarskoe Selo, Tobolsk and Ekaterinburg. There were exercise books that had belonged to Marie and Anastasia, together with a pencil case and bell that had belonged to the Tsarevich. There were even menus from Tobolsk; the last one read: 'Lunch: borshch, hazel-hen [partridge] with rice. Dinner: veal garnished and macaroni'.

However, according to Dmitri, Father Nicholas remained reluctant to discuss his memories. It was not until his very last few years that he opened up, talking at length both to the art students in Robert Street and to Beattie. 'He was impressed by the harmony of the family. He never heard a harsh word. Most importantly, he saw how they were all strengthened by their religious faith,' comments Beattie.

On 24 March 1963, two months after his 87th birthday, Father Nicholas died in St Pancras Hospital.

He had been admitted after suffering a minor stroke. He retained his fighting spirit to the end: Charles remembers being told that his adoptive grandfather suffered his final, fatal stroke after becoming exasperated with a nurse.

A funeral service at Ennismore Gardens was followed by an emotional leave-taking in the chapel at Marston Street. Katkov was among the coffin-bearers as Father Nicholas was carried to his final resting-place at Headington Cemetery.

Days after his death, Beattie and Bishop Kallistos – then Timothy Ware – paid a visit to George in Robert Street. They were concerned about what would happen to Father Nicholas' possessions. George led the two young men to Father Nicholas' bedroom. He pointed out an icon hanging over the bed which had been given to Father Nicholas by the Imperial family. He told them it had been dull until about three days before Father Nicholas' death, when it had begun to shine.

'The icon *was* shining...' Beattie says with a small smile, '...I draw no conclusion.'

Beattie's feeling at the time was that Father

Nicholas was, at last, where he wanted to be. 'In his simple way, Father Nicholas had been looking forward to seeing the Imperial family again. I felt there was a sense of completion.'

ACKNOWLEDGEMENTS

There are many people I want to thank.

Charles Gibbes Paveliev shared his memories of his adoptive grandfather with me. He lent photographs, letters and diaries, all of which he packed up and brought over from France, where he now lives.

His brother, Andrew Gibbes, spent time reminiscing on the telephone from his home in Canada. Doreen Gibbs, a niece, was helpful in offering her family's perspective on Father Nicholas.

As one of Father Nicholas' last close friends, Dmitri Kornhardt provided testimony that was invaluable; during our morning together, he took me to Bartlemas Chapel and, movingly, to Father Nicholas' grave in Oxford. Bishop Kallistos of Diokleia and David Beattie, who both encountered him in their youth, spent hours sharing their thoughts and recollections with me.

Dr Tanya Joyce offered fond memories of Father Nicholas from her childhood. Prof Elisabeth Koutaissoff gave an incisive perspective on Father Nicholas as a priest. John Stuart combined his own memory of Father Nicholas with a useful list of memoirs that mention his early life. Nicholas Garland reminisced about his time as one of Father Nicholas' student lodgers.

Lena Snow kindly put me in touch with several people in Oxford who had known Father Nicholas. Marina Fennell was also extremely helpful. The author, Christine Benagh, and Steven Tomlinson of the Bodleian Library both helped me gain access to further letters. Zena Dickinson of the Wernher Foundation offered information about the Gibbes collection as well as helping me in my search for Charles Gibbes Paveliev. Terry Moore, a former colleague of Charles, made numerous inquiries on my account.

Lastly, I would like to thank my husband Craig and our children, Tallulah and Silas, for their forbearance in keeping their eyes from glazing over at the mention of either of the two names that recurred – and still recur – in our house: Sydney Gibbes and Father Nicholas.

In case of difficulty in purchasing any Short Books
title through normal channels, please contact
BOOKPOST Tel: 01624 836000
Fax: 01624 837033
email: bookshop@enterprise.net
www.bookpost.co.uk
Please quote ref. 'Short Books'